Oracle Initialization
Parameters
Pocket Reference

Oracle Initialization Parameters
Pocket Reference

David C. Kreines

O'REILLY®

Beijing · Cambridge · Farnham · Köln · Paris · Sebastopol · Taipei · Tokyo

Oracle Initialization Parameters Pocket Reference
by David C. Kreines

Copyright © 2004 O'Reilly Media, Inc. All rights reserved.
Printed in the United States of America.

Published by O'Reilly Media, Inc., 1005 Gravenstein Highway North,
Sebastopol, CA 95472.

O'Reilly books may be purchased for educational, business, or sales
promotional use. Online editions are also available for most titles
(*safari.oreilly.com*). For more information, contact our corporate/
institutional sales department: (800) 998-9938 or *corporate@oreilly.com*.

Editor:	Deborah Russell
Production Editor:	Jamie Peppard
Cover Designer:	Emma Colby
Interior Designer:	David Futato

Printing History:

August 2004: First Edition.

0-596-00770-1
[C]

Contents

Oracle Initialization Parameters Pocket Reference

Introduction

Oracle is designed to be a very flexible and configurable system. These qualities are absolute necessities for a database that can run on dozens of different hardware platforms in a multitude of configurations, supporting an almost infinite variety of applications and users. In order to achieve the needed flexibility, Oracle must provide the database administrator (DBA) with a simple method of specifying certain operational characteristics of the database in a clear and consistent manner. DBAs specify most of these characteristics by setting and resetting values for the database *initialization parameters*, commonly referred to as *INIT.ORA parameters*. The goal is to set these parameters in a way that maximizes database performance while minimizing DBA maintenance and resulting downtime.

The purpose of this pocket reference is to provide a clear and concise summary of the initialization parameters available in Oracle. This book is not a tutorial; rather, it provides a quick and easy way of finding the information you need when you need it.

Because Oracle Corporation is constantly improving and updating their database product, there are several versions of Oracle commonly in use today. For that reason, I've included initialization parameters for the following versions of Oracle:

Oracle8*i*
Oracle9*i*
Oracle Database 10*g*

Where appropriate, I note when a parameter was discontinued or a new parameter was added. For example, the parameter ACTIVE_INSTANCE_COUNT is available for use beginning with Oracle9i. The parameter ALWAYS_ANTI_JOIN can be used in Oracle8i but becomes obsolete effective with Oracle9i. This information will be especially crucial if you upgrade to a new version.

Each initialization parameter controls a specific aspect of the Oracle server. Together, all the parameters combine to shape the generic Oracle database technology to fit the particular needs of your organization and/or platform.

The following is a typical initialization file for a general-purpose installation of Oracle:

```
DB_NAME = "ORAC"
DB_DOMAIN = oraserver
INSTANCE_NAME = ORAC
SERVICE_NAMES = ORAC.oraserver

DB_FILES = 1024
DB_BLOCK_SIZE = 8192

COMPATIBLE = 9.2.0
SORT_AREA_SIZE = 65536
SORT_AREA_RETAINED_SIZE = 65536

CONTROL_FILES = (/disk0/oracle/oradata/ORAC/control01.ctl,
                 /disk1/oracle/oradata/ORAC/control02.ctl,
                 /disk2/oracle/oradata/ORAC/control03.ctl)

OPEN_CURSORS = 100
CURSOR_SHARING = similar

MAX_ENABLED_ROLES = 30
DB_FILE_MULTIBLOCK_READ_COUNT = 8
DB_BLOCK_BUFFERS = 2048

SHARED_POOL_SIZE = 19728640
LARGE_POOL_SIZE = 614400
JAVA_POOL_SIZE = 25971520

LOG_CHECKPOINT_INTERVAL = 10000
```

```
LOG_CHECKPOINT_TIMEOUT = 1800

PROCESSES = 200
PARALLEL_MAX_SERVERS = 5
LOG_BUFFER = 32768
MAX_DUMP_FILE_SIZE = 10240   # Limit the size of this file
GLOBAL_NAMES = true

ORACLE_TRACE_COLLECTION_NAME = ""
BACKGROUND_DUMP_DEST = /disk1/Oracle/admin/ORAC/bdump
RESOURCE_MANAGER_PLAN = system_plan
USER_DUMP_DEST = /disk1/oracle/admin/ORAC/udump
TRACEFILE_IDENTIFIER = ORAC

REMOTE_LOGIN_PASSWORDFILE = exclusive
OS_AUTHENT_PREFIX = ""

PLSQL_COMPILER_FLAGS = debug
UNDO_MANAGEMENT = auto
```

The filenames shown in this example are appropriate for
Unix. If you are running another operating system—Windows, for example—you will need to replace these names
with the appropriate filename formats for your system.

This example shows only some of the basic parameters in the
initialization file. In an operational system, you would probably include additional parameters; you would typically also
include comments (e.g., see MAX_DUMP_FILE_SIZE) that
describes the specific effects of the parameters in your environment and the revision history of changes to the parameters.

Most of this Pocket Reference consists of a comprehensive,
alphabetical list of initialization parameters. Preceding the
quick reference are several sections describing the various
categories of parameters and the files used to store them.

Acknowledgments

Thanks to all those who helped in the conception and production of this book. Thanks to Rick Greenwald, my coauthor on *Oracle in a Nutshell* (O'Reilly), to Jonathan Gennick for suggestions and technical review, to the staff at O'Reilly for handling the production of this book, and last, but certainly not least, to my editor, Debby Russell, who pushed the project and me.

Conventions

The following typographical conventions are used in this book:

UPPERCASE
Indicates an Oracle parameter name or keyword.

Italic
Indicates a filename or directory; also used for emphasis and the introduction of new technical terms.

`Constant width`
Used for parameter syntax and code examples.

`Constant width italic`
Indicates a value you need to supply when specifying a parameter.

[ ] In syntax models, square brackets enclose optional items.

{ } In syntax models, curly brackets enclose a set of items from which you must choose only one.

| In syntax models, a vertical bar separates the items enclosed in curly brackets, such as {TRUE | FALSE}.

Parameter Files and Types

The name and location of the database initialization parameter file on your system depends on the Oracle version and the operating system you are running, as described in the following sections.

INIT.ORA: The Initialization File

In Oracle releases prior to Oracle9*i*, initialization parameters are specified in a file referred to as the *INIT.ORA* file. The actual file name is usually in the form init*sid*.ora, where *sid* is the SID, or system identifier, for your particular Oracle instance. The SID is a unique name used to identify a particular instance. Typically, the *INIT.ORA* file is found in the *$ORACLE_HOME/dbs* directory.

TIP

Refer to the Oracle documentation for the default location of this file for your particular operating system.

Be sure to store the *INIT.ORA* file in a location where it is accessible to the client that is starting the database.

Because the *INIT.ORA* file is a simple text file, it can be modified using any ASCII editor. However, be careful not to use a word processing program such as Microsoft Word to edit the *INIT.ORA* file; Oracle cannot read such files. If you must use Word to create the file, save the file as a plain ASCII text file.

Parameters are typically entered into the file one parameter and value per line, as shown in the earlier example. Comments may be added after a parameter or on their own line, but are always preceded by a # character. For example:

```
# The following line contains a comment
DB_FILE_MULTIBLOCK_READ_COUNT = 8   # Do not change
```

SPFILE: The Server Parameter File

Oracle introduced the concept of the server parameter file in Oracle9*i*. This file, known as an *SPFILE*, differs from the standard *INIT.ORA* file in a number of ways:

- It is a binary file, rather than a text-based file.
- It is stored on the server, rather than on a client machine.
- It can maintain changes to parameter values over the shutdown and startup of an instance.

This last difference is the important one: if your database is running under Oracle9i or later, any changes you make to configuration parameters via the ALTER SYSTEM statement are saved as part of the permanent configuration file. That means that, by default, if you change any of your database parameter values for tuning purposes, you don't have to make the same change in the *INIT.ORA* file to retain the new values.

You can also make dynamic changes to parameters without making them a part of the *SPFILE*; to do so, include the SCOPE clause in the ALTER SYSTEM statement, using the following syntax:

```
ALTER SYSTEM SET parameter_name = parameter_value
   SCOPE = {MEMORY | SPFILE | BOTH};
```

Even if you are running Oracle9i and later, you can still use a local *INIT.ORA* file by specifying the location of that file with a PFILE=*name* clause in the STARTUP statement. For example:

```
STARTUP PFILE=/home/oracle/myinit.ora
```

Oracle9i and Oracle Database 10g also provide a simple way to migrate the parameters in an existing *INIT.ORA* file to the binary *SPFILE* for an instance. You can copy the *INIT.ORA* file to the server machine (if it's not already there) and issue the following command from SQL*Plus, substituting the complete actual pathname for *pathname*:

```
CREATE SPFILE FROM PFILE='pathname/initsid.ora';
```

By default, the *SPFILE* is located in the *$ORACLE_HOME/ dbs* directory. The SPFILE parameter, which you can specify in your *INIT.ORA* file, allows you to point to a nondefault location for the *SPFILE*; simply include a line such as the following in your file:

```
SPFILE=$ORACLE_HOME/dbs/spfile.ora;
```

WARNING

Although the *SPFILE* looks like a plain text file, it is very important to realize that the *SPFILE* cannot be directly edited. If you edit your *SPFILE* (with a text editor, for example), your next attempt to start your database will fail.. You will be unable to start your database unless you have created a backup *SPFILE* or *INIT.ORA* file (which is a good practice for just this reason).

Dynamically Modifiable Parameters

While most initialization parameters are static, taking their values from the initialization file as it exists at the time of database startup, some may be dynamically modified while the instance is up and the database is open.

Dynamic modification is different from dynamic storage of a changed value in the *SPFILE*. In all versions of Oracle, you can dynamically modify many settings using the ALTER SYSTEM or ALTER SESSION statement. Starting with Oracle9*i*, these changes may also be dynamically stored in the *SPFILE*, depending on the value of the SCOPE clause of the ALTER statement.

WARNING

Remember that if you use an *INIT.ORA* file, dynamic changes to parameters will never be saved to the *INIT. ORA* file: you must edit the file yourself (or recreate it from the *SPFILE*).

The Quick Reference portion of this book shows which initialization parameters may be dynamically modified. In the individual parameter descriptions in that section, the "Dynamic" entry indicates whether the parameter is dynamically modifiable, as well as how it may be modified (via ALTER SYSTEM, ALTER SESSION, or both).

Parameters by Function

The Quick Reference portion of this book lists initialization parameters alphabetically. In the following sections, however, they are grouped in a number of functional categories; within each category, they are listed alphabetically. The parameters are arranged this way because you will frequently use a group of parameters to control a particular area of operation, such as auditing or job management, or you may need to know all the parameters that relate to a particular area of database configuration. These sections simply list the parameters; for detailed descriptions, consult the Quick Reference. Table 1 lists the functional categories; the few parameters that don't fit into any of the categories are listed in the section "Miscellaneous Parameters."

Table 1. Categories of initialization parameters

Auditing	Backup and recovery
Clustered databases	Cursors
Database links	Distributed operations and Heterogeneous Services
II/O and space management	Java
Jobs	Licenses
Locking and transactions	Logging and archiving
Memory management	Names
National Language Support	Optimization and performance
Parallel execution	Parameters
PL/SQL	Remote sites
Rollback/undo/redo management	Security
Shared Server/Multi-Threaded Server	Standby databases
Storage	System operations
Tracing	Miscellaneous parameters

Auditing

The following parameters shape how auditing is performed in the Oracle database:

    AUDIT_FILE_DEST
    AUDIT_TRAIL
    TRANSACTION_AUDITING

Backup and Recovery

The following parameters shape and control the options and operations of backup and recovery. See the descriptions of related parameters in the "Logging and Archiving" and "Rollback/Undo/RedoManagement" sections.

    BACKUP_DISK_IO_SLAVES
    BACKUP_TAPE_IO_SLAVES
    DB_RECOVERY_FILE_DEST
    DB_RECOVERY_FILE_DEST_SIZE
    FAST_START_IO_TARGET
    FAST_START_MTTR_TARGET
    FAST_START_PARALLEL_ROLLBACK
    RECOVERY_PARALLELISM

Clustered Databases

The following parameters apply to either Oracle Parallel Server (prior to Oracle9*i*) or Real Application Clusters (beginning with Oracle9*i*):

    CLUSTER_DATABASE
    CLUSTER_DATABASE_INSTANCES
    CLUSTER_INTERCONNECTS
    DRS_START
    GC_DEFER_TIME
    GC_FILES_TO_LOCKS
    GC_LCK_PROCS
    GC_RELEASABLE_LOCKS
    GC_ROLLBACK_LOCKS
    GCS_SERVER_PROCESSES
    INSTANCE_GROUPS
    INSTANCE_NAME

INSTANCE_NUMBER
INSTANCE_TYPE
LM_LOCKS
LM_RESS
LOG_FILE_NAME_CONVERT
MAX_COMMIT_PROPAGATION_DELAY
PARALLEL_SERVER

Cursors

The following parameters shape the use of cursors:

CURSOR_SHARING
CURSOR_SPACE_FOR_TIME
OPEN_CURSORS
SERIAL_REUSE
SESSION_CACHED_CURSORS

Database Links

The following parameters concern the use of database links
(DB links) to remote databases:

DBLINK_ENCRYPT_LOGIN
OPEN_LINKS
OPEN_LINKS_PER_INSTANCE

Distributed Operations and Heterogeneous Services

The following parameters control distributed operations and
Heterogeneous Services (HS) used with Oracle:

COMMIT_POINT_STRENGTH
DB_UNIQUE_NAME
DISTRIBUTED_TRANSACTIONS
HS_AUTOREGISTER
MAX_TRANSACTION_BRANCHES

I/O and Space Management

The following parameters shape and control I/O operations and space management:

    DB_BLOCK_CHECKING
    DB_BLOCK_SIZE
    DB_FILE_DIRECT_IO_COUNT
    DB_FILE_MULTIBLOCK_READ_COUNT
    DB_FILES
    DISK_ASYNCH_IO
    HASH_MULTIBLOCK_IO_COUNT
    RESUMABLE_TIMEOUT

Java

The following parameters apply to the use of Java in the database:

    JAVA_MAX_SESSIONSPACE_SIZE
    JAVA_POOL_SIZE
    JAVA_SOFT_SESSIONSPACE_LIMIT

Jobs

The following parameters apply to jobs and the job queue:

    JOB_QUEUE_INTERVAL
    JOB_QUEUE_PROCESSES

Licenses

The following parameters apply to Oracle licensing:

    LICENSE_MAX_SESSIONS
    LICENSE_MAX_USERS
    LICENSE_SESSIONS_WARNING

Locking and Transactions

The following parameters change the ways that Oracle handles locking behavior and transactions:

    DDL_WAIT_FOR_LOCKS
    DML_LOCKS
    ENQUEUE_RESOURCES
    ROW_LOCKING
    TRANSACTIONS
    TRANSACTION_PER_ROLLBACK_SEGMENT

Logging and Archiving

The following parameters shape and control logging and archiving. See also the related parameters in the "Rollback/Undo/Redo Management" section.

    ARCHIVE_LAG_TARGET
    CPU_COUNT
    DB_CREATE_ONLINE_LOG_DEST_*n*
    FAL_CLIENT
    FAL_SERVER
    LOG_ARCHIVE_CONFIG
    LOG_ARCHIVE_DEST
    LOG_ARCHIVE_DEST_*n*
    LOG_ARCHIVE_DEST_STATE_*n*
    LOG_ARCHIVE_DUPLEX_DEST
    LOG_ARCHIVE_FORMAT
    LOG_ARCHIVE_LOCAL_FIRST
    LOG_ARCHIVE_MAX_PROCESSES
    LOG_ARCHIVE_MIN_SUCCEED_DEST
    LOG_ARCHIVE_START
    LOG_ARCHIVE_TRACE
    REMOTE_ARCHIVE_ENABLE

Memory Management

The following parameters shape and control the way memory is allocated and used:

    BITMAP_MERGE_AREA_SIZE
    BUFFER_POOL_KEEP

BUFFER_POOL_RECYCLE
CREATE_BITMAP_AREA_SIZE
DB_CACHE_ADVICE
DB_nK_CACHE_SIZE
DB_BLOCK_BUFFERS
DB_CACHE_SIZE
DB_KEEP_CACHE_SIZE
DB_RECYCLE_CACHE_SIZE
HASH_AREA_SIZE
HI_SHARED_MEMORY_ADDRESS
LARGE_POOL_SIZE
LOCK_SGA
OBJECT_CACHE_MAX_SIZE_PERCENT
OBJECT_CACHE_OPTIMAL_SIZE
PGA_AGGREGATE_TARGET
PRE_PAGE_SGA
SGA_MAX_SIZE
SGA_TARGET
SHARED_MEMORY_ADDRESS
SHARED_POOL_RESERVED_SIZE
SHARED_POOL_SIZE
SORT_AREA_RETAINED_SIZE
SORT_AREA_SIZE
STREAMS_POOL_SIZE
USE_INDIRECT_DATA_BUFFERS
WORKAREA_SIZE_POLICY

Names

The following parameters control and assign names to different files and objects:

DB_CREATE_FILE_DEST
DB_DOMAIN
DB_FILE_NAME_CONVERT
DB_NAME
DB_UNIQUE_NAME
ENT_DOMAIN_NAME
GLOBAL_NAMES
SERVICE_NAMES

National Language Support

The following parameters control the use of National Language Support (NLS) character sets:

    NLS_CALENDAR
    NLS_COMP
    NLS_CURRENCY
    NLS_DATE_FORMAT
    NLS_DATE_LANGUAGE
    NLS_DUAL_CURRENCY
    NLS_ISO_CURRENCY
    NLS_LANGUAGE
    NLS_LENGTH_SEMANTICS
    NLS_NUMERIC_CHARACTERS
    NLS_SORT
    NLS_TERRITORY
    NLS_TIMESTAMP_FORMAT
    NLS_TIMESTAMP_TZ_FORMAT

Optimization and Performance

The following parameters apply to the Oracle optimizer and to various Oracle performance features:

    BLANK_TRIMMING
    CREATE_STORED_OUTLINES
    HASH_JOIN_ENABLED
    OPTIMIZER_FEATURES_ENABLE
    OPTIMIZER_INDEX_CACHING
    OPTIMIZER_INDEX_COST_ADJ
    OPTIMIZER_MAX_PERMUTATIONS
    OPTIMIZER_MODE
    OPTIMIZER_PERCENT_PARALLEL
    OPTIMIZER_SEARCH_LIMIT
    PARTITION_VIEW_ENABLED
    QUERY_REWRITE_ENABLED
    QUERY_REWRITE_INTEGRITY
    READ_ONLY_OPEN_DELAYED
    SKIP_UNUSABLE_INDEXES
    SQLTUNE_CATEGORY
    STAR_TRANSFORMATION_ENABLED
    TIMED_STATISTICS

Parallel Execution

The following parameters configure parallel execution:

    PARALLEL_ADAPTIVE_MULTI_USER
    PARALLEL_AUTOMATIC_TUNING
    PARALLEL_BROADCAST_ENABLED
    PARALLEL_DEFAULT_MAX_INSTANCES
    PARALLEL_EXECUTION_MESSAGE_SIZE
    PARALLEL_INSTANCE_GROUP
    PARALLEL_MAX_SERVERS
    PARALLEL_MIN_PERCENT
    PARALLEL_MIN_SERVERS
    PARALLEL_THREADS_PER_CPU

Parameters

The following parameters point to other parameter files:

    IFILE
    SPFILE

PL/SQL

The following parameters apply to the use of the PL/SQL language:

    PLSQL_CODE_TYPE
    PLSQL_COMPILER_FLAGS
    PLSQL_DEBUG
    PLSQL_LOAD_WITHOUT_COMPILE
    PLSQL_NATIVE_C_COMPILER
    PLSQL_NATIVE_LIBRARY_DIR
    PLSQL_NATIVE_LIBRARY_SUBDIR_COUNT
    PLSQL_NATIVE_LINKER
    PLSQL_NATIVE_MAKE_UTILITY
    PLSQL_OPTIMIZE_LEVEL
    PLSQL_V2_COMPATIBILITY
    PLSQL_WARNINGS
    SMTP_OUT_SERVER
    SQLTUNE_CATEGORY
    UTL_FILE_DIR

Remote Sites

The following parameters control how you interact with remote sites:

    REMOTE_DEPENDENCIES_MODE
    REMOTE_LISTENER
    REMOTE_OS_AUTHENT
    REMOTE_OS_ROLES

Rollback/Undo/Redo Management

The following parameters apply to the management and use of rollback segments, undo tablespaces, and redo logs:

    DB_FLASHBACK_RETENTION_TARGET
    LOG_BLOCK_CHECKSUM
    LOG_BUFFER
    LOG_CHECKPOINT_INTERVAL
    LOG_CHECKPOINT_TIMEOUT
    LOG_CHECKPOINTS_TO_ALERT
    MAX_ROLLBACK_SEGMENTS
    ROLLBACK_SEGMENTS
    TRANSACTIONS_PER_ROLLBACK_SEGMENT
    UNDO_MANAGEMENT
    UNDO_RETENTION
    UNDO_SUPPRESS_ERRORS
    UNDO_TABLESPACE

Security

The following parameters affect how security is enforced for Oracle:

    LDAP_DIRECTORY_ACCESS
    MAX_ENABLED_ROLES
    O7_DICTIONARY_ACCESSIBILITY
    OS_AUTHENT_PREFIX
    OS_ROLES
    RDBMS_SERVER_DN
    REMOTE_LOGIN_PASSWORDFILE
    SQL92_SECURITY

Shared Server/Multi-Threaded Server

The following parameters control and shape the operation of the Shared Server (beginning with Oracle9*i*) and Multi-Threaded Server (MTS) (prior to Oracle9*i*):

    CIRCUITS
    DISPATCHERS
    MAX_DISPATCHERS
    MAX_SHARED_SERVERS
    MTS_CIRCUITS
    MTS_DISPATCHERS
    MTS_MAX_DISPATCHERS
    MTS_MAX_SERVERS
    MTS_SERVERS
    MTS_SERVICE
    MTS_MULTIPLE_LISTENERS
    SHARED_SERVER_SESSIONS

Standby Databases

The following parameters apply to the use of standby databases:

    ACTIVE_INSTANCE_COUNT
    LOCK_NAME_SPACE
    STANDBY_ARCHIVE_DEST
    STANDBY_FILE_MANAGEMENT
    STANDBY_PRESERVES_NAMES

Storage

The following parameters apply to Oracle's management of storage and to the use of the Automated Storage Management (ASM) facility, introduced with Oracle Database 10*g*:

    ASM_DISKGROUPS
    ASM_DISKSTRING
    ASM_POWER_LIMIT
    FILEIO_NETWORK_ADAPTERS
    INSTANCE_TYPE
    RESUMABLE_TIMEOUT

System Operations

The following parameters apply to various system processes, the overall operation of Oracle, dump files, and control files:

    BACKGROUND_CORE_DUMP
    BACKGROUND_DUMP_DEST
    CONTROL_FILE_RECORD_KEEP_TIME
    CONTROL_FILES
    CORE_DUMP_DEST
    DB_BLOCK_CHECKSUM
    DB_BLOCK_LRU_LATCHES
    DB_BLOCK_MAX_DIRTY_TARGET
    DB_WRITER_PROCESSES
    DBWR_IO_SLAVES
    MAX_DUMP_FILE_SIZE
    PROCESSES
    RESOURCE_LIMIT
    RESOURCE_MANAGER_PLAN
    SESSION_MAX_OPEN_FILES
    SESSIONS
    SHADOW_CORE_DUMP
    THREAD

Tracing

The following parameters affect the operation of Oracle Trace:

    ORACLE_TRACE_COLLECTION_NAME
    ORACLE_TRACE_COLLECTION_PATH
    ORACLE_TRACE_COLLECTION_SIZE
    ORACLE_TRACE_ENABLE
    ORACLE_TRACE_FACILITY_NAME
    ORACLE_TRACE_FACILITY_PATH
    SQL_TRACE
    TRACE_ENABLED
    TRACEFILE_IDENTIFIER
    USER_DUMP_DEST

Miscellaneous Parameters

The following parameters do not fit any previous categories:

ALWAYS_ANTI_JOIN
AQ_TM_PROCESSES
COMPATIBLE
COMPLEX_VIEW_MERGING
EVENT
FIXED_DATE
LOCAL_LISTENER
LOGMNR_MAX_PERSISTENT_SESSIONS
REPLICATION_DEPENDENCY_TRACKING

Parameter Quick Reference

The remaining pages of this Pocket Reference describe the Oracle initialization parameters. Parameters are listed in alphabetical order. Parameter names are shown here in uppercase for readability, but you can specify parameters in upper-, lower-, or mixed-case in the parameter file.

TIP

In addition to the initialization parameters listed in this chapter that apply to most Oracle systems, a handful of additional parameters are specific to particular hardware platforms or operating systems. These parameters are documented in the installation guide, user guide, and/or release notes for your release of Oracle.

For each parameter, I include one or more of the following entries, as appropriate:

Value or Values
  Indicates valid value(s) for the parameter. This may be a single value, one of several values, a range of values, or a type of values (string, integer, etc.). You can specify the following abbreviations in many parameter values when referencing quantities of memory or disk storage: K (kilobytes), M (megabytes), G (gigabytes). Note that strings do not normally require quotes; if quotes are required for a specific parameter value, this is noted.

Default

Indicates default value for the parameter. Note that Oracle does not provide default values for all parameters.

Dynamic

Specifies the statement (ALTER SESSION, ALTER SYSTEM) that modifies a parameter that can be dynamically modified. If this entry is not included, the parameter may not be dynamically modified.

Syntax

Indicates syntax for specifying the parameter; syntax is included only for complicated parameter assignments.

Keywords

Lists keywords (if any) you may specify in setting the parameter's value.

Description

Describes the parameter and its usage.

Limitations on support

Indicates parameters that are not supported in all versions of Oracle covered in this book (Oracle8*i*, Oracle9*i*, and Oracle Database 10*g*). The parameter description notes whether a parameter is new in a particular version or is applicable only in an earlier version of the database. If this entry is not included, the parameter is supported for all the Oracle versions described in this book.

ACTIVE_INSTANCE_COUNT

Value: Positive integer

Default: None

In a cluster of exactly two instances, a value of 1 indicates that the first instance started is the primary instance, while the second instance acts as a standby. Any other value is ignored. New with Oracle9*i*.

ALWAYS_ANTI_JOIN

Value: NESTED_LOOPS | MERGE | HASH

Default: NESTED_LOOPS

Sets the type of antijoin that the Oracle Server uses. Obsolete with Oracle9*i*.

Keywords

NESTED_LOOPS
   Server uses a nested loop antijoin algorithm.

MERGE
   Server uses the sort merge antijoin algorithm.

HASH
   Server uses the hash antijoin algorithm to evaluate the subquery.

AQ_TM_PROCESSES

Value: 0 | 1

Default: 0

Dynamic: ALTER SYSTEM

If this parameter is set to 1, a one-time manager process is created to monitor the messages. If the parameter is not specified or is set to 0, the manager is not created.

ARCHIVE_LAG_TARGET

Value: 0 or 60 – 7200

Default: 0

Dynamic: ALTER SYSTEM

Specifies the time (in seconds) that will elapse before a log switch is forced. A value of 0 indicates that the time-based thread advance feature is disabled. New with Oracle9*i*.

ASM_DISKGROUPS

Value: List of strings

Default: None

Dynamic: ALTER SYSTEM

Specifies a list of one or more names (separated by a comma) of disk groups to be mounted by an Automatic Storage Management (ASM) instance at instance startup or when the ALTER DISKGROUP ALL MOUNT statement is issued.

ASM automatically adds a disk group to this parameter when a disk group is successfully mounted and automatically removes the disk group when it is dismounted (unless the dismount is at instance shutdown). New with Oracle Database 10g.

ASM_DISKSTRING

Value: List of strings

Default: NULL

Dynamic: ALTER SYSTEM

Specifies one or more operating system dependent discovery strings (separated by a comma) that are used by Automatic Storage Management to limit the set of disks considered for discovery. When a new disk is added to a disk group, each ASM instance that has the disk group mounted must be able to discover the new disk using the value provided.

In most cases, the default value will be sufficient. Using a more restrictive value may reduce the time required for ASM to perform discovery, and thus improve disk group mount time or the time for adding a disk to a disk group. It may be necessary to dynamically change ASM_DISKSTRING before adding a disk so that the new disk will be discovered. Note that if the new value cannot be used to discover a disk that is in a disk group that is already mounted, an attempt to dynamically modify ASM_DISKSTRING is rejected, and the old value is retained. New with Oracle Database 10g.

ASM_POWER_LIMIT

Value: 1–11

Default: 1

Dynamic: ALTER SYSTEM, ALTER SESSION

Specifies the maximum power on an Automatic Storage Management instance for rebalancing the disks. Higher values result in faster rebalancing, while lower values take longer but result in lower system resource consumption. If the POWER clause of a rebalance operation is specified, the ASM_POWER_LIMIT value is not used.

AUDIT_FILE_DEST

Value: Valid directory

Default: $ORACLE_HOME/RDBMS/AUDIT

Specifies the fully qualified directory in which auditing files are stored.

AUDIT_TRAIL

Value: NONE | FALSE | DB | TRUE | OS

Default: NONE

Enables or disables the writing of rows to the audit trail. The SQL AUDIT statements can set auditing options regardless of how this parameter is set.

Keywords

NONE
> Audited records are not written.

FALSE
> Supported for backward compatibility. Same as NONE.

DB
> Enables system-wide auditing and causes audited records to be written to the database audit trail (the SYS.AUD$ table).

TRUE
> Supported for backward compatibility. Same as DB.

OS
> Enables system-wide auditing and causes audited records to be written to the operating system's audit trail

BACKGROUND_CORE_DUMP

Value: FULL | PARTIAL

Default: FULL

Specifies how the System Global Area (SGA) is handled during a core dump. If FULL, the SGA is dumped as part of the generated core file. If PARTIAL, the SGA is not dumped as part of the generated core file.

BACKGROUND_DUMP_DEST

Value: String

Default: Operating system dependent

Dynamic: ALTER SYSTEM

Specifies the fully qualified directory name where debugging trace files for the background processes (LGWR, DBWR, and so on) are written during Oracle operations.

BACKUP_DISK_IO_SLAVES

Value: 0 – 15

Default: 0

Specifies the number of I/O slaves used by the Recovery Manager to back up, copy, or restore data to disk. Obsolete with Oracle9i.

BACKUP_TAPE_IO_SLAVES

Value: TRUE | FALSE

Default: FALSE

Dynamic: ALTER SYSTEM DEFERRED

Specifies whether I/O slaves are used by the Recovery Manager to back up, copy, or restore data to tape.

BITMAP_MERGE_AREA_SIZE

Value: Operating system dependent

Default: 1000000

Specifies the amount of memory used to merge bitmaps retrieved from a range scan of the index. A larger value should improve performance because the bitmap segments must be sorted before being merged into a single bitmap.

BLANK_TRIMMING

Value:　　　TRUE | FALSE

Default:　　FALSE

A value of TRUE allows the data assignment of a source character string/variable to a destination character column/variable even though the source length is longer than the destination length, if the additional length comprises all blanks. A value of FALSE disallows this type of data assignment.

BUFFER_POOL_KEEP

Value:　　　Integer | BUFFERS:integer | LRU_LATCHES:integer

Default:　　None

Specifies the number of buffers (of size DB_BLOCK_BUFFER) to be set aside as a KEEP buffer pool. Optionally specifies the number of LRU latches to be allocated to the KEEP buffer pool.

Beginning with Oracle9i, Oracle recommends that you use the DB_KEEP_CACHE_SIZE parameter instead of BUFFER_POOL_KEEP.

If this parameter is specified, DB_KEEP_CACHE_SIZE cannot be specified, or an error will result.

BUFFER_POOL_RECYCLE

Value:　　　Integer | BUFFERS:integer | LRU_LATCHES:integer

Default:　　None

Specifies the number of buffers (of size DB_BLOCK_BUFFER) to be set aside as a RECYCLE buffer pool. Optionally specifies the number of LRU latches to be allocated to the RECYCLE buffer pool.

Beginning with Oracle9i, Oracle recommends that you use the DB_RECYCLE_CACHE_SIZE parameter instead of BUFFER_POOL_RECYCLE.

If this parameter is specified, DB_RECYCLE_CACHE_SIZE cannot be specified, or an error will result.

CIRCUITS

Value:　　　Integer

Default:　　See description

Specifies the total number of virtual circuits available for network connections in a Shared Server environment. The default is the value of SESSIONS if Shared Server is in use; otherwise, the default is 0. New with Oracle9*i*.

CLUSTER_DATABASE

Value: TRUE | FALSE

Default: FALSE

Specifies whether Real Application Clusters (RAC) is enabled. Must be set to TRUE for all instances in a Real Application Cluster. New with Oracle9*i*.

CLUSTER_DATABASE_INSTANCES

Value: Positive integer

Default: 1

Specifies the number of instances participating in a Real Application Cluster. Should be set to the same value in each instance. New with Oracle9*i*.

CLUSTER_INTERCONNECTS

Value: One or more valid IP addresses, separated by colons (e.g., 192.168.1.11:192.168.1.23)

Default: None

Specifies additional interconnect IP addresses in a Real Application Cluster, in order to improve performance in large clusters. New with Oracle9*i*.

COMMIT_POINT_STRENGTH

Value: 0–255

Default: Operating system dependent

Specifies a value that determines the commit point site in a distributed transaction. The node in the transaction with the highest value for COMMIT_POINT_STRENGTH is the commit point site. A database's commit point strength should be set relative to the amount of critical shared data in the database.

COMPATIBLE

Value: 7.3.0 – current Oracle release

Default: Current Oracle release (e.g., 9.2.0)

Allows the use of a new release while at the same time guaranteeing backward compatibility with an earlier release. Some features of the current release may be restricted.

When you use the standby database feature, this parameter must have the same value on both databases, and the value must be 7.3.0.0.0 or higher.

COMPLEX_VIEW_MERGING

Value: TRUE | FALSE

Default: FALSE

Specifies whether complex view merging should be enabled. Obsolete with Oracle9i.

CONTROL_FILE_RECORD_KEEP_TIME

Value: 0 – 365

Default: 7

Dynamic: ALTER SYSTEM

Specifies the minimum age (in days) that a record that is in the circularly reusable section of the control file must be before it can be reused. If a new record needs to be added to a reusable section, and the oldest record has not aged enough, the record section expands. If this parameter is set to 0, reusable sections never expand, and records are reused as needed. Here are the names of the reusable sections of the control file:

    ARCHIVED LOG
    BACKUP CORRUPTION
    BACKUP DATAFILE
    BACKUP PIECE
    BACKUP REDO LOG
    BACKUP SET
    COPY CORRUPTION
    DATAFILE COPY

DELETED OBJECT
LOGHISTORY
OFFLINE RANGE

CONTROL_FILES

Value: 1– 8 filenames

Default: operating system dependent

Specifies one or more names of control files, separated by commas.

CORE_DUMP_DEST

Value: String

Default: $ORACLE_HOME/dbs

Dynamic: ALTER SYSTEM

Specifies the fully qualified directory name to which core dump files are written.

CPU_COUNT

Value: 0 – unlimited

Default: 0 or actual number of CPUs

Specifies the number of CPUs available to Oracle. Oracle uses this setting to set the default value of the LOG_SIMULTANEOUS_ COPIES parameter. On single-CPU computers, the value of CPU_ COUNT is 0.

On most platforms, Oracle automatically sets the value of CPU_ COUNT to the number of CPUs available to the Oracle instance. If there is heavy contention for latches, change the value of LOG_ SIMULTANEOUS_COPIES to twice the number of CPUs available, but do not change the value of CPU_COUNT.

CREATE_BITMAP_AREA_SIZE

Value: Operating system dependent

Default: 8 MB

Specifies the amount of memory allocated for bitmap creation. The default value is 8 MB, and a larger value might lead to faster index creation. If the cardinality (the number of unique values) of the index is very small, you can set a small value for this parameter.

CREATE_STORED_OUTLINES

Value: TRUE | FALSE | category_name

Default: FALSE

Dynamic: ALTER SYSTEM, ALTER SESSION

Specifies whether Oracle automatically creates and stores an outline for each query submitted during the session. A value of TRUE enables automatic outline creation for subsequent queries in the same session. These outlines receive a unique system-generated name and are stored in the DEFAULT category. If a query already has an outline defined for it in the DEFAULT category, that outline will remain, and a new outline will not be created. A value of FALSE disables automatic outline creation during the session. A value of *category_name* has the same behavior as TRUE except that an outline created is stored in the *category_name* category (e.g., CREATE_STORED_OUTLINE=trial). New with Oracle Database 10*g*.

CURSOR_SHARING

Value: SIMILAR | EXACT | FORCE

Default: None

Dynamic: ALTER SYSTEM, ALTER SESSION

Specifies the way that SQL statements can share cursors in memory. New with Oracle9*i*.

Keywords

SIMILAR

Specifies that SQL that is identical except for literals will share the same cursor in memory unless the literals affect the meaning of the SQL statement or the degree to which the execution plan is optimized.

EXACT
Specifies that SQL must be identical to share the same cursor in memory.

FORCE
Specifies that SQL that is the same except for literals will share the same cursor.

CURSOR_SPACE_FOR_TIME

Value: TRUE | FALSE

Default: FALSE

Controls the use of memory used to store cursors. If this parameter is set to TRUE, the database uses more space for cursors to save time. Because the shared SQL areas never leave memory while they are in use, this parameter should be set to TRUE only when the shared pool is large enough to hold all open cursors simultaneously. Setting this parameter to TRUE also retains the private SQL area allocated for each cursor between executes instead of discarding it after cursor execution, which saves cursor allocation and initialization time.

DB_BLOCK_BUFFERS

**Value
(Oracle8/8i):**   4 – operating system dependent

Default: 50

**Value
(Oracle9i/10g):**   50 – operating system dependent

Default: 48M / DB_BLOCK_SIZE

Specifies the number of database buffers available in the buffer cache. This is one of the primary parameters that contribute to the total memory requirements of the SGA on the Oracle instance. The DB_BLOCK_BUFFERS parameter, together with the DB_BLOCK_SIZE parameter, determines the total size of the buffer cache.

Beginning with Oracle9i, Oracle recommends that you use DB_CACHE_SIZE instead of DB_BLOCK_BUFFERS.

DB_BLOCK_CHECKING

Value: TRUE | FALSE

Default: FALSE

Dynamic: ALTER SYSTEM, ALTER SESSION

Specifies whether data blocks are checked for corruption before being written. Setting this parameter to TRUE results in a performance penalty of up to 10%, so use it with caution. New with Oracle8i.

DB_BLOCK_CHECKSUM

Value: TRUE | FALSE

Default: FALSE

Dynamic: ALTER SYSTEM

Specifies whether DBWR and the direct loader can calculate a checksum and store it in the cache header of every data block when writing it to disk. Setting DB_BLOCK_CHECKSUM to TRUE can incur additional performance overhead. Set this parameter to TRUE only if you are advised to do so by Oracle Support.

DB_BLOCK_LRU_LATCHES

Value: 1 – number of CPUs

Default: CPU_COUNT / 2

Specifies the maximum number of LRU latch sets. If the parameter is not set, Oracle calculates a value that is usually adequate. Increase this value only if misses are higher than 3% in V$LATCH. Obsolete with Oracle9i.

DB_BLOCK_MAX_DIRTY_TARGET

Value: 100 – all buffers in the cache

Default: All buffers in the cache

Specifies the number of buffers that can be dirty (modified and different from what is on disk). If the number of dirty buffers in a buffer cache exceeds this value, DBWR writes out buffers in order to try to keep the number of dirty buffers below the specified value. This parameter can influence the amount of time it takes to perform instance recovery because recovery is related to the number of buffers that are dirty at the time of the crash. The smaller the value of this parameter, the faster the instance recovery. Setting this value to 0 disables the writing of buffers for incremental checkpointing purposes; all other write activity continues as is. Obsolete with Oracle9i.

DB_BLOCK_SIZE

Value: 2048–32768 but may be less depending on operating system

Default: Operating system dependent

Specifies the size (in bytes) of Oracle database blocks. The value for DB_BLOCK_SIZE when the database is created determines the size of the blocks, and at all other times the value must be set to the original value. In a RAC environment, this parameter affects the maximum value of the FREELISTS storage parameter for tables and indexes, because Oracle uses one database block for each FREELIST block.

This value can be set only at database creation time and must not be changed afterward.

DB_CACHE_ADVICE

Value: ON | OFF | READY

Default: OFF

Dynamic: ALTER SYSTEM

Specifies how statistics-gathering used for predicting database performance with different cache sizes will be performed. If this parameter is set to OFF and then changed to ON using the ALTER SYSTEM statement, an error is likely to occur, because adequate memory will not have been allocated. Use the READY setting to allow this parameter to be changed to ON at a later time. New with Oracle9i.

Keywords

ON
    Cache advisory is turned on and statistics are gathered.

OFF
> Cache advisory is turned off, and no memory is allocated for the gathering of statistics.

READY
> Cache advisory is turned off, but memory is allocated for statistics.

DB_CACHE_SIZE

Value: Integer [K | M | G]

Default: 48M

Dynamic: ALTER SYSTEM

Specifies the size of the DEFAULT buffer pool in the SGA buffers with the primary block size (specified by DB_BLOCK_SIZE). New with Oracle9i.

DB_CREATE_FILE_DEST

Value: String

Default: None

Dynamic: ALTER SYSTEM, ALTER SESSION

Specifies the fully qualified directory name where datafiles, control files, and online log files will be created (e.g., DB_CREATE_FILE_DEST=/disk01/oradata). The directory specified must already exist and must have sufficient permissions to allow Oracle to create files in it. New with Oracle9i.

DB_CREATE_ONLINE_LOG_DEST_n

Value: String

Dynamic: ALTER SYSTEM, ALTER SESSION

Specifies the fully qualified directory name where online log files and control files will be created. To provide fault tolerance, you should specify this parameter at least twice. The directory specified must already exist and have sufficient permissions to allow Oracle to create files in it. New with Oracle9i.

Syntax

```
DB_CREATE_ONLINE_LOG_DEST_n = directory
```

Keywords

n Integer between 1 and 5 that specifies the multiplexed file instance.

directory

Specifies the name of a directory that will contain one member of each online redo log group and one control file.

DB_DOMAIN

Value: String

Default: WORLD

Specifies the extension components of a global database name, consisting of valid identifiers separated by periods (e.g., us. oracle.com). The database domain name may be composed of alphabetic characters, numbers, and underscore (_) and pound (#) characters. The total length of the string cannot exceed 128 characters.

DB_FILE_DIRECT_IO_COUNT

Value: Operating system dependent

Default: 64

Specifies the number of blocks to be used for I/O operations performed by backup, restore, or direct path read and write functions. The I/O buffer size is a product of DB_FILE_DIRECT_IO_COUNT and DB_BLOCK_SIZE and cannot exceed the maximum I/O size for the platform. Obsolete with Oracle9*i*.

DB_FILE_MULTIBLOCK_READ_COUNT

Value: 1 – operating system dependent

Default: 8

Dynamic: ALTER SYSTEM, ALTER SESSION

Specifies the maximum number of blocks read in one I/O operation during a sequential scan. Batch environments typically have values for this parameter in the range of 4 to 16. Decision support/data warehouse database environments tend to benefit from maximizing the value for this parameter. The actual maximum varies by operating system; it is always less than or equal to the operating system's maximum I/O size expressed as Oracle blocks (maximum I/O size/DB_BLOCK_SIZE).

DB_FILE_NAME_CONVERT

Value: List of strings

Default: None

Specifies how Oracle converts the filename of a new datafile on the primary database to a filename on the standby database. The file must exist and be writable on the standby database, or the recovery process will halt with an error. The value of this parameter is two strings: the first string is the pattern found in the datafile names on the primary database; the second string is the pattern found in the datafile names on the standby database (e.g., DB_FILE_NAME_CONVERT = '/disk01/data/db1_','/disk01/data/db2_'). New with Oracle9*i*.

DB_FILES

Value: Number of datafiles currently in the database minus the value specified in the MAXDATAFILES clause the last time CREATE DATABASE or CREATE CONTROLFILE was executed

Default: Operating system dependent

Specifies the maximum number of database files that can be opened for this database. This parameter should be set for the maximum number of files, subject to operating system constraints, that will ever be specified for the database, including files to be added via the ADD DATAFILE statement. If the value of DB_FILES is increased, all instances accessing the database must be shut down and restarted before the new value can take effect.

DB_FLASHBACK_RETENTION_TARGET

Value: $0 - 2^{32} - 1$

Default: 1440

Dynamic: ALTER SYSTEM

Specifies how far back (in minutes) the database may be flashed back, depending on how much flashback data Oracle has kept in the flash recovery area. New with Oracle Database 10g.

DB_KEEP_CACHE_SIZE

Value: Integer [K | M | G]

Default: 0

Dynamic: ALTER SYSTEM

Specifies the number of buffers (of size DB_BLOCK_SIZE) in the KEEP buffer pool. New with Oracle9i.

DBLINK_ENCRYPT_LOGIN

Value: TRUE | FALSE

Default: FALSE

Specifies whether attempts to connect to other Oracle servers through database links should use encrypted passwords. If TRUE, and the connection fails, Oracle does not reattempt a failed connection. If FALSE, Oracle reattempts the connection using an unencrypted version of the password.

DB_NAME

Value: String

Default: NULL

Specifies the name of the database (up to eight characters). If specified, it must be the same as the name specified in the CREATE DATABASE statement. If it is not specified, a database name must appear on either the STARTUP or the ALTER DATABASE MOUNT command line for each instance of the Parallel Server. Multiple instances must have the same value, or else the same value must be specified in STARTUP OPEN db_name or ALTER DATABASE db_name MOUNT. Note that the value provided for this parameter is case sensitive.

DB_nK_CACHE_SIZE

Value: 2 | 4 | 8 | 16 | 32

Default: Not configured

Dynamic: ALTER SYSTEM

Specifies the size of cache for *n*K buffers, when DB_BLOCK_SIZE is set to a value different from *n*K. Cannot be less than the minimum block size and cannot exceed the maximum block size on the platform. New with Oracle9*i*.

DB_RECOVERY_FILE_DEST

Value: Directory | disk group

Default: None

Dynamic: ALTER SYSTEM

Specifies the default location for the flash recovery area, which contains multiplexed copies of current control files and online redo logs, as well as archived redo logs, flashback logs, and RMAN backups. If this parameter is specified, DB_RECOVERY_FILE_ DEST_SIZE must also be specified. New with Oracle Database 10*g*.

DB_RECOVERY_FILE_DEST_SIZE

Value: Integer [K | M | G]

Default: None

Dynamic: ALTER SYSTEM

Specifies the limit (in bytes) on the total space to be used by target database recovery files created in the flash recovery area. New with Oracle Database 10*g*.

DB_RECYCLE_CACHE_SIZE

Value: Integer [K | M | G]

Default: 0

Dynamic: ALTER SYSTEM

Specifies the number of buffers (of size DB_BLOCK_SIZE) in the RECYCLE buffer pool. New with Oracle9*i*.

DB_UNIQUE_NAME

Value: String

Default: Value of DB_NAME

Specifies a globally unique name for the database. Databases with the same DB_NAME within the same DB_DOMAIN must have a unique DB_UNIQUE_NAME, and every database's DB_UNIQUE_NAME must be unique within the enterprise. The value can be up to 30 characters and is case insensitive. New with Oracle Database 10*g*.

DDL_WAIT_FOR_LOCKS

Value: TRUE | FALSE

Default: FALSE

Dynamic: ALTER SYSTEM, ALTER SESSION

Specifies whether DDL statements wait and complete (TRUE) or time out (FALSE).

DBWR_IO_SLAVES

Value: 0 – operating system dependent

Default: 0

Specifies the number of I/O slaves used by the DBW0 process to perform writes to disk and to simulate asynchronous I/O on platforms that do not support asynchronous I/O or that implement it inefficiently. This parameter is valid only when DB_WRITER_PROCESSES is set to 1. If specified, it forces DB_WRITER_PROCESSES to be set to 1.

DB_WRITER_PROCESSES

Value: 1 – 20

Default: 1

Specifies the number of DB writer processes created for an instance.

DISK_ASYNCH_IO

Value: TRUE | FALSE

Default: TRUE

Controls whether I/O to datafiles, control files, and log files is asynchronous. If a platform does not support asynchronous I/O to disk, this parameter has no effect. If DISK_ASYNCH_IO is set to FALSE, the DBWR_IO_SLAVES parameter should be set to a nonzero value in order to simulate asynchronous I/O.

DISPATCHERS

Value: Quoted string (see description)

Default: None

Dynamic: ALTER SYSTEM

Configures dispatcher processes in a Shared Server environment. New with Oracle9*i*.

Syntax

```
DISPATCHERS ='{ (PROTOCOL = protocol)
 | (ADDRESS = address)
 | (DESCRIPTION = description)
}
[({DISPATCHERS = integer
   | SESSIONS = integer
   | CONNECTIONS = integer
   | TICKS = seconds
   | POOL = {1 | ON | YES | TRUE | BOTH |
             ({IN | OUT} = integer) | 0 | OFF | NO |
             FALSE | integer}
   | MULTIPLEX = {1 | ON | YES | TRUE |
                 0 | OFF | NO | FALSE | BOTH | IN | OUT}
   | LISTENER = tnsname
   | SERVICE = service
   | INDEX = integer
})]'
```

Keywords

protocol
    Network protocol for the dispatcher.

address
    Network protocol address for the dispatcher.

description
    Network description for the dispatcher.

DISPATCHERS
    Initial number of dispatchers.

SESSIONS
    Maximum number of network sessions per dispatcher.

CONNECTIONS
    Maximum number of network connections per dispatcher.

TICKS
    Length of a network tick (in seconds).

POOL
    Controls connection pooling. ON, YES, TRUE, and BOTH
    specify connection pooling for IN and OUT network connec-
    tions. NO, OFF, and FALSE specify no connection pooling
    for IN and OUT network connections. IN and OUT specify
    connection pooling for their respective network connections.
    An integer by itself indicates the timeout for both types of
    connections. You can include an integer with IN or OUT,
    such as (IN = 20)(OUT = 10), to specify the ticks for each
    direction. The default timeout is 10.

MULTIPLEX
    Enables network session multiplexing for both IN and OUT
    connections with 1, ON, YES, TRUE, or BOTH. Disables
    with 0, NO, OFF, or FALSE. IN and OUT enable multi-
    plexing in their respective directions.

LISTENER
    Network name of an address, or an address list for the Oracle
    Net listener that will register the dispatcher.

SERVICE
    Service name the dispatchers register with the listeners.

INDEX
    Identifies a particular dispatcher when used with the ALTER
    SYSTEM SET DISPATCHERS statement. Note that 0 is the
    index base.

For example, the following is a simple use of this parameter to
create three dispatchers for the TCP protocol:

```
DISPATCHERS = '(PROTOCOL=TCP)(DISPATCHERS=3)'
```

DISTRIBUTED_TRANSACTIONS

Value:　　　　0 – TRANSACTIONS

Default:　　　TRANSACTIONS * 25

Specifies the maximum number of distributed transactions in which this database can concurrently participate. The value of this parameter cannot exceed the value of the TRANSACTIONS parameter. If DISTRIBUTED_TRANSACTIONS is set to 0, no distributed transactions are allowed, and the recovery process does not start when the instance starts up.

DML_LOCKS

Value:　　　　0 | 20 – unlimited

Default:　　　4 * TRANSACTIONS

Specifies the maximum number of DML locks; include one for each table modified in a transaction. The value should equal the grand total of locks on tables currently referenced by all users. If the value is set to 0, enqueues are disabled and performance is slightly increased. However, you will not be able to use DROP TABLE, CREATE INDEX, or explicit lock statements such as LOCK TABLE IN EXCLUSIVE MODE. Multiple instances must all have positive values or must all be 0.

DRS_START

Value:　　　　TRUE | FALSE

Default:　　　FALSE

Dynamic:　　ALTER SYSTEM

Specifies whether the disaster recovery process (DRMON) is started. Should be specified only if the instance will be part of a disaster recovery configuration.

ENQUEUE_RESOURCES

Value:　　　　10 – unlimited

Default:　　　Derived from SESSIONS

Sets the number of resources that can be concurrently locked by the Lock Manager. For fewer than 4 sessions, the default value is 20; for 4 to 10 sessions, the default value is ((SESSIONS - 3) * 5) + 20; and for more than 10 sessions, it is ((SESSIONS - 10) * 2) + 55. If ENQUEUE_RESOURCES is explicitly set to a value higher than DML_LOCKS + 20, the value provided is used. If there are many tables, the value may be increased. Allow one per resource, regardless of the number of sessions or cursors using that resource. Increase the value if Oracle returns an error specifying that enqueues are exhausted.

ENT_DOMAIN_NAME

Value: String

Default: None

Specifies the enterprise domain name (e.g., acme_mfg). Applies only to Oracle8*i*.

EVENT

Value: Provided by Oracle Support

Default: None

Used to debug the system. Set this parameter only if you are advised to do so by Oracle Support.

FAL_CLIENT

Value: String

Default: None

Dynamic: ALTER SYSTEM

Specifies the name of the Fetch Archive Log client used by the FAL service (e.g., prod.world). New with Oracle9*i*.

FAL_SERVER

Value: String

Default: None

Dynamic: ALTER SYSTEM

Specifies the name of the Fetch Archive Log server for a standby database and must point to the FAL server (e.g., stby.world). New with Oracle9i.

FAST_START_IO_TARGET

Value: 0 | 1000 – all buffers in the cache

Default: All buffers in the cache

Dynamic: ALTER SYSTEM

Specifies the number of buffer I/O operations expected to be used during crash or instance recovery. Lower values cause the DB writer process to write dirty buffers to disk more often in order to keep buffer I/O at recovery within the target set, at the expense of overall performance. The value 0 disables fast-start check-pointing. New with Oracle8i and available only with Enterprise Edition.

With Oracle9i, Oracle recommends that you use FAST_START_MTTR_TARGET instead of this parameter.

FAST_START_MTTR_TARGET

Value: 0 – 3600

Default: 0

Dynamic: ALTER SYSTEM

Specifies the number of seconds expected to be used during crash or instance recovery. Works like FAST_START_IO_TARGET, but ignored if that parameter or LOG_CHECKPOINT_INTERVAL is specified. New with Oracle9i.

FAST_START_PARALLEL_ROLLBACK

Value: HIGH | LOW | FALSE

Default: LOW

Dynamic: ALTER SYSTEM

Specifies the maximum number of processes that perform parallel rollback. FALSE disables parallel rollback; LOW sets the number to 2 * CPU_COUNT; and HIGH sets the number to 4 * CPU_COUNT. New with Oracle9*i*.

FILEIO_NETWORK_ADAPTERS

Value: adapter_name [,adapter_name]

Default: None

Specifies the name(s) (separated by commas) of one or more network adapters that can access the disk storage where the database files reside in network attached storage. *adapter_name* is a fully qualified address name of the network card that can be accessed through the hostname database or via the Network Information Service (e.g., ad1.acme.com). New with Oracle Database 10*g*.

FIXED_DATE

Value: String

Default: None

Dynamic: ALTER SYSTEM

Specifies a constant date that SYSDATE always returns instead of the current date. The format of the date is:

    YYYY-MM-DD-HH24:MI:SS

Also accepts the default Oracle date format, without a time. Specify the value with double quotes (not single quotes) or without quotes; for example:

    FIXED_DATE = "30-NOV-04"

or:

    FIXED_DATE = 30-NOV-04

GC_DEFER_TIME

Value: Any positive integer

Default: 10

Dynamic: ALTER SYSTEM

Specifies the time, in hundredths of a second, that the server waits before responding to forced-write requests for hot blocks from other instances. The default value means that the feature is disabled. Obsolete with Oracle9i.

GC_FILES_TO_LOCKS

Value: See description

Default: None

An Oracle Parallel Server parameter that controls the mapping of Parallel Cache Management (PCM) locks to datafiles. The parameter can be used to limit the number of locks used per datafile and to specify that each lock should cover a set of contiguous blocks. If this parameter is specified, Oracle disables the Cache Fusion processing feature of Oracle9i Real Application Clusters. Multiple instances must have identical values.

Syntax

```
GC_FILES_TO_LOCKS = '{file_list=lock_count[!blocks][EACH]}[:]..
.'
```

Keywords

file_list

>One or more datafiles listed by their file numbers, or ranges of file numbers, separated by commas.

lock_count

>Number of PCM locks assigned to *file_list*. If *lock_count* is set to 0, then fine-grained locking is used for these files.

!blocks

>Optionally indicates the number of contiguous blocks covered by one lock.

EACH

>Optionally specifies that each datafile in *file_list* is assigned a separate set of *lock_count* PCM locks; the default is noncontiguous blocks.

For example, you can assign 400 locks to file 1 and 200 locks to file 2 as follows:

```
GC_FILES_TO_LOCKS = '1=300:2=100'
```

GC_LCK_PROCS

Value: 1 – 10, or 0 for a single instance running in exclusive mode

Default: 1

Sets the number of background lock processes (LCK0 through LCK9) for an instance in a Parallel Server. The default of 1 is normally sufficient, but the value can be increased if the distributed lock request rate saturates the lock process. Multiple instances must have identical values.

GC_RELEASABLE_LOCKS

Value: 50 – unlimited

Default: value of DB_BLOCK_BUFFERS

Specifies a value used to allocate space for fine-grained locking. There is no maximum value, except as imposed by memory restrictions. Specific to Oracle Parallel Server in shared mode. Obsolete with Oracle9i.

GC_ROLLBACK_LOCKS

Value: 1 – unlimited

Default: 0 – 128=32!8REACH

Specifies, for each rollback segment, the number of distributed locks available for simultaneously modified rollback segment blocks for Oracle Parallel Server. The default is adequate for most applications. Each instance must have identical values. Obsolete with Oracle9i.

Syntax

```
GC_ROLLBACK_LOCKS = 'rs_list = lock_count[!blocks][R][EACH][:...]'
```

Keywords

rs_list

One or more rollback segments listed by their segment numbers or ranges of segment numbers, separated by commas.

lock_count

Number of PCM locks assigned to *rs_list*.

!blocks
> Number of contiguous blocks covered by one lock. The default is noncontiguous blocks.

R
> Indicates that these locks are releasable and are drawn as needed from the pool of releasable locks.

EACH
> Indicates that each rollback segment in *rs_list* is assigned a separate set of *lock_count* PCM locks.

GCS_SERVER_PROCESSES

Value: 1 – 20

Default: See description

Specifies the initial number of server processes in Global Cache Service to serve the inter-instance traffic among Real Application Clusters instances. If CLUSTER_DATABASE is set to TRUE, then the value of this parameter defaults to 2; otherwise it defaults to 0. New with Oracle Database 10*g*.

GLOBAL_NAMES

Value: TRUE | FALSE

Default: FALSE

Dynamic: ALTER SESSION, ALTER SYSTEM

Specifies whether a database link is required to have the same name as the database to which it connects. If FALSE, no check is performed. If TRUE, forces the use of consistent naming conventions for databases and links. If distributed processing is used, set GLOBAL_NAMES to TRUE to ensure a unique identifying name for each database in a networked environment.

HASH_AREA_SIZE

Value: 0 – operating system dependent

Default: 2 SORT_AREA_SIZE

Dynamic: ALTER SESSION

Specifies the maximum amount of memory (in bytes) to be used for hash joins.

HASH_JOIN_ENABLED

Value: TRUE | FALSE

Default: TRUE

Dynamic: ALTER SESSION

Specifies whether the optimizer will consider using a hash join.

HASH_MULTIBLOCK_IO_COUNT

Value: Operating system dependent

Default: 1

Dynamic: ALTER SESSION

Specifies how many sequential blocks a hash join reads and writes in one I/O. When operating in Multi-Threaded Server mode, this parameter is ignored, and a value of 1 is used. The maximum value is always less than the operating system's maximum I/O size expressed as Oracle blocks. This parameter strongly affects performance because it controls the number of partitions into which the input is divided. Obsolete with Oracle9*i*.

HI_SHARED_MEMORY_ADDRESS

Value: Integer address

Default: 0

Specifies the starting address of the SGA. A value of 0 causes the SGA address to default to a system-specific address. On 64-bit platforms, this parameter specifies the high-order 32 bits of the address; SHARED_MEMORY_ADDRESS specifies the low-order 32 bits.

HS_AUTOREGISTER

Value: TRUE | FALSE

Default: TRUE

Dynamic: ALTER SYSTEM

Specifies whether automatic self-registration of Heterogeneous Services agents is enabled. Oracle recommends setting this parameter to TRUE because overhead will thus be reduced when establishing subsequent connections through the same agent. New with Oracle8*i*.

IFILE

Value: String containing valid filename

Default: None

Specifies the name of another parameter file to be embedded within the current parameter file. Up to three levels of nesting can be used. You can include multiple parameter files in one parameter file by listing IFILE several times with different values.

INSTANCE_GROUPS

Value: List of strings

Default: None

Assigns the current instance to the specified groups that are separated by commas (e.g., group_1,group_2). This is a Real Application Clusters/Oracle Parallel Server parameter. See the PARALLEL_INSTANCE_GROUP parameter.

INSTANCE_NAME

Value: String containing instance name

Default: Current instance system identifier (SID)

Specifies the name of the instance. Primarily useful in Real Application Clusters or Oracle Parallel Server, where it may be desirable to specify a particular instance with which to connect to the database. New with Oracle8*i*.

INSTANCE_NUMBER

Value: 1 – maximum number of instances specified in CREATE DATABASE statement

Default: Lowest available number

Specifies a unique number that maps the instance to one group of free space lists for each table created with the storage option FREELIST GROUPS. The INSTANCE option of the ALTER TABLE ALLOCATE EXTENT statement assigns an extent to a particular group of free lists. If INSTANCE_NUMBER is set to the value specified for the INSTANCE option, the instance uses that extent for inserts and updates that expand rows. INSTANCE_NUMBER is an Oracle Parallel Server parameter. Multiple instances must have different values.

INSTANCE_TYPE

Value: RDBMS | ASM

Default: RDBMS

Specifies whether the instance is a database instance or an Automatic Storage Management instance. New with Oracle Database 10g.

JAVA_MAX_SESSIONSPACE_SIZE

Value: 0 – 4 GB

Default: 0

Specifies the maximum amount of session space (in bytes) that will be made available to a Java program executing on the server. New with Oracle8i.

WARNING

If the user session attempts to allocate more memory than specified here, the Java Virtual Manager (JVM) generates an out-of-memory condition and the session is killed.

JAVA_POOL_SIZE

Value: 1000000 – 1000000000

Default: 20000

Specifies the size of the Java pool (in bytes) in the SGA. New with Oracle8i.

JAVA_SOFT_SESSIONSPACE_LIMIT

Value: 0 – 4 GB

Default: 0

Specifies the amount (in bytes) of Java memory that can be used in a session before a warning is generated in a trace file. New with Oracle8i.

JOB_QUEUE_INTERVAL

Value: 1 – 3600

Default: 60

Specifies the interval (in seconds) between wake-ups for the SNP*n* background processes of the instance. Oracle8 and Oracle8i only.

JOB_QUEUE_PROCESSES

Value: 0 – 1000

Default: 0

Dynamic: ALTER SYSTEM

Specifies the maximum number of background processes per instance that can be created for the execution of jobs.

LARGE_POOL_SIZE

Value: 300K – 2 GB or higher (maximum is operating system dependent)

Default: 0

Specifies the size (in bytes) of the large pool allocation heap. If specified, the minimum size is 600K (300K in Oracle8) or LARGE_POOL_MIN_ALLOC, whichever is larger. The value of the parameter can be specified in bytes, megabytes (M), or kilobytes (K). The default of 0 means that no large pool is allocated.

LDAP_DIRECTORY_ACCESS

Value: NONE | PASSWORD | SSL

Default: None

Dynamic: ALTER SYSTEM

Specifies whether Oracle refers to the Oracle Internet Directory (OID) for user authentication information. If a value is supplied, then this parameter specifies how users are authenticated. New with Oracle Database 10g.

Keywords

None

> If this parameter is not supplied, Oracle does not refer to the OID for Enterprise User Security information.

PASSWORD

> Oracle tries to connect to the enterprise directory service using the database password stored in the database wallet. If that fails, the OID connection fails, and the database cannot retrieve enterprise roles and schema mappings upon enterprise user login.

SSL

> Oracle tries to connect to the OID using the Secure Sockets Layer (SSL).

LICENSE_MAX_SESSIONS

Value: 0 – number of session licenses

Default: 0

Specifies the maximum number of concurrent user sessions allowed simultaneously. When this limit is reached, only users with the RESTRICTED SESSION privilege can connect to the server, and users who cannot connect receive a warning message indicating that the system has reached maximum capacity.

Usage licensing and user licensing should not be enabled concurrently; you must always set either LICENSE_MAX_SESSIONS or LICENSE_MAX_USERS to zero. If this parameter is set to a nonzero number, LICENSE_SESSIONS_WARNING should also be set.

LICENSE_MAX_USERS

Value: 0 – number of user licenses

Default: 0

Specifies the maximum number of users that can be created in the database. When this limit is reached, additional users cannot be created. Multiple instances should have the same value.

LICENSE_SESSIONS_WARNING

Value: 0 – LICENSE_MAX_SESSIONS

Default: 0

Specifies a warning limit on the number of concurrent user sessions. When this limit is reached, additional users can connect, but Oracle writes a message in the alert file for each new connection. Users with the RESTRICTED SESSION privilege who connect after the limit is reached receive a warning message stating that the system is nearing its maximum capacity.

LM_LOCKS

Value: 512 – available shared memory

Default: 12000

Specifies the number of locks that are configured for the Lock Manager when running Parallel Server. The number of locks is represented by the following equation:

$$L = R + (R * (N - 1)) / N$$

where:

R is the number of resources
N is the total number of nodes
L is the total number of locks

Multiple instances must have the same value. Obsolete with Oracle9*i*.

LM_RESS

Value: 256 − available shared memory

Default: 6000

Oracle Parallel Server parameter that controls the number of resources that can be locked by each Lock Manager instance. The value specified for LM_RESS should be much less than 2 * DML_LOCKS plus an overhead of about 20 locks. Multiple instances must have the same value. Obsolete with Oracle9*i*.

LOCAL_LISTENER

Value: String

Default: See description

Identifies "local" listeners so that they can complete client connections to dedicated servers. Specifies the network name of either a single address or an address list, which must the same machine as the instance. When present, LOCAL_LISTENER overrides MTS_LISTENER_ADDRESS and MTS_MULTIPLE_LISTENERS. For example:

```
(ADDRESS_LIST =
  (ADDRESS = (PROTOCOL=TCP) (HOST=prd1) (PORT=1526))
  (ADDRESS = (PROTOCOL=IPC) (KEY=db1))
)
```

The default value for this parameter is:

```
(ADDRESS_LIST = (ADDRESS = (PROTOCOL=TCP) (HOST=localhost)
        (PORT=1521))
  (ADDRESS = (PROTOCOL=IPC)
  (KEY= dbname)))
```

LOCK_NAME_SPACE

Value: 8 characters maximum, no special characters allowed

Default: None

Specifies the namespace (e.g., clone_db) that the Distributed Lock Manager (DLM) uses to generate lock names.

LOCK_SGA

Value: TRUE | FALSE

Default: FALSE

Specifies whether the entire SGA is locked into real (physical) memory. Specify TRUE if there is a potential for the SGA's being swapped to disk because swapping can significantly degrade performance.

LOG_ARCHIVE_CONFIG

Value: See description

Default: 'SEND, RECEIVE, NODG_CONFIG'

Dynamic: ALTER SYSTEM

Specifies whether the sending and receiving of redo logs to and from remote destinations is enabled, and specifies the unique database names (DB_UNIQUE_NAME) for each database in the Data Guard configuration. New with Oracle Database 10g.

Syntax

```
LOG_ARCHIVE_CONFIG = '
[ SEND | NOSEND ]
[ ,RECEIVE | NORECEIVE ]
[ ,DG_CONFIG=(remote_db_unique_name1
     [, ... remote_db_unique_name9) | NODG_CONFIG ] '
```

Keywords

SEND
    Enables the sending of redo logs to remote destinations.

NOSEND
    Disables the sending of redo logs to remote destinations.

RECEIVE
    Enables the receipt of remotely archived redo logs.

NORECEIVE
Disables the receipt of remotely archived redo logs.

DG_CONFIG
Specifies a list of up to nine unique database names (defined with the DB_UNIQUE_NAME initialization parameter) for all the databases in the Data Guard configuration.

NODG_CONFIG
Eliminates the list of service provider names previously specified with the DG_CONFIG option.

LOG_ARCHIVE_DEST

Value: String

Default: Operating system dependent

Dynamic: ALTER SYSTEM

Specifies the name of a fully qualified directory or tape device to be used as a destination when archiving redo log files. Note that archiving to tape is not supported on all operating systems.

Oracle recommends that if the Enterprise Edition of Oracle8*i* or Oracle9*i* is used, you set LOG_ARCHIVE_DEST_*n* instead of LOG_ARCHIVE_DEST.

LOG_ARCHIVE_DEST_*n*

Value: See description

Default: None

Dynamic: ALTER SYSTEM, ALTER SESSION

Specifies up to 10 archived log destinations. This parameter is valid for only the Oracle8*i* or Oracle9*i* Enterprise Edition. If you use this parameter, you must not use LOG_ARCHIVE_DEST.

Syntax

```
LOG_ARCHIVE_DEST_n = {SERVICE = service | LOCATION = location}
    [AFFIRM | NOAFFIRM]
    [ALTERNATE = destination | NOALTERNATE]
    [ARCH | LGWR]
    [DB_UNIQUE_NAME | NODB_UNIQUE_NAME]
    [DELAY[= minutes] | NODELAY]
    [DEPENDENCY = destination | NODEPENDENCY]
    [MANDATORY | OPTIONAL]
    [MAX_FAILURE = count | NOMAX_FAILURE]
    [NET_TIMEOUT = seconds | NONET_TIMEOUT]
    [QUOTA_SIZE = blocks | NOQUOTA_SIZE]
    [QUOTA_USED = blocks | NOQUOTA_USED]
    [REGISTER | NOREGISTER]
    [REOPEN = seconds | NOREOPEN]
    [SYNC = {PARALLEL | NOPARALLEL} | ASYNC=blocks]
    [TEMPLATE | NOTEMPLATE]
    [VALID_FOR = redo_log_type, database_role]
    [VERIFY | NOVERIFY]
```

Keywords

n   Number from 1 to 10 that identifies the destination.

SERVICE = *service*

Specifies the name of a network service that transmits the archived log file to a standby instance.

LOCATION = *location*

Specifies a local filesystem destination. If multiple LOG_ARCHIVE_DEST_*n* parameters are supplied, at least one must specify a LOCATION.

MANDATORY

Specifies that archiving to the destination must succeed before the redo log file can be reused.

NET_TIMEOUT

Specifies the time (in seconds) that must elapse before a network timeout occurs. NONET_TIMEOUT means no network timeout will occur.

OPTIONAL

Specifies that successful archiving to the destination is not required before the redo log file can be reused. This is the default.

REOPEN = *seconds*

Specifies the number of seconds that must pass before the destination can be used for archiving after an error. The default is 300 seconds.

TIP

Additional keywords are available with this parameter (see the previous syntax diagram), but those keywords are related to Oracle Data Guard, and are not commonly used. For more detailed information on these keywords, refer to the *Oracle Data Guard Concepts and Administration Manual*.

LOG_ARCHIVE_DEST_STATE_n

Value: ENABLE | DEFER

Default: ENABLE

Dynamic: ALTER SYSTEM, ALTER SESSION

Specifies whether the corresponding LOG_ARCHIVE_DEST_n is available. You can use a LOG_ARCHIVE_DEST_n parameter only with the corresponding LOG_ARCHIVE_DEST_n parameter.

LOG_ARCHIVE_DUPLEX_DEST

Value: String

Default: NULL

Dynamic: ALTER SYSTEM

Specifies a fully qualified directory name or device name to be used as a second archive destination. This *duplex archive destination* can be either a must-succeed or a best-effort archive destination, depending on how many archive destinations must succeed (see the LOG_ARCHIVE_MIN_SUCCEED_DEST parameter).

Oracle recommends that you set LOG_ARCHIVE_DEST_*n* instead of this parameter if the Enterprise Edition is used: do not use both.

LOG_ARCHIVE_FORMAT

Value: String containing filename format

Default: Operating system dependent

Specifies the filename format for archiving redo log files while running in ARCHIVELOG mode. The string filename generated from this format is appended to the directory string specified in the LOG_ARCHIVE_DEST parameter.

The following variables can be used in the format:

%a Activation ID.

%d Database ID.

%r Resetlogs ID, which causes unique names to be constructed for archived log files across multiple incarnations of the database.

%s Log sequence number.

%S Log sequence number, zero filled.

%t Thread number, which must be specified when using RAC.

%T Thread number, zero-filled.

The default is operating system dependent but is usually *%t_%s. dbf*. Using uppercase letters (for example, %S) for a variable causes the value to be a fixed length padded to the left with zeros.

TIP

In a RAC environment, the thread number must be specified, using either %t or %T.

LOG_ARCHIVE_LOCAL_FIRST

Value: TRUE | FALSE

Default: TRUE

Dynamic: ALTER SYSTEM

Specifies when the archiver processes transmit redo data to remote standby database destinations. New with Oracle Database 10g.

Keywords

TRUE

>   Directs the ARCn process to transmit redo data after the online redo log file has been completely and successfully archived to at least one local destination. Note that because the online redo log files are archived locally first, the LGWR process reuses the online redo log files much earlier than would be possible if the log field were archived to the standby database concurrently with the local destination.

FALSE

>   Directs the ARCn process to transmit redo data at the same time the online redo log file is archived to the local destinations. This results in redo data being promptly dispatched to the remote standby database destination.

If LOG_ARCHIVE_LOCAL_FIRST is set to TRUE, it is not used on a physical standby database nor any database for which the following attributes have been specified in the LOG_ARCHIVE_DEST_n initialization parameter:

>   MANDATORY
>   LOCAL
>   DEPENDENCY (or any database destination that is the target of a DEPENDENCY attribute)

Also, if LOG_ARCHIVE_LOCAL_FIRST is set to TRUE, it is ignored during operations, for example, during a switchover, that require synchronized archival operations. If the destination was explicitly configured to use the log writer process (by specifying the LGWR attribute in the LOG_ARCHIVE_DEST_n initialization parameter), but for some reason the log writer process becomes unable to archive to the destination, Data Guard reverts to the ARCn process to complete archival operations with the default behavior, even if LOG_ARCHIVE_LOCAL_FIRST is set to FALSE.

LOG_ARCHIVE_MAX_PROCESSES

Value: 1 – 10

Default: 1

Dynamic: ALTER SYSTEM

Specifies the maximum number of archiver processes, named ARC0 through ARC9, that Oracle initially creates. New with Oracle8*i*.

LOG_ARCHIVE_MIN_SUCCEED_DEST

Value: 1 – 10

Default: 1

Dynamic: ALTER SYSTEM, ALTER SESSION

Specifies the minimum number of archive log destinations that must succeed when automatic archiving is enabled. If LOG_ARCHIVE_DEST_*n* is specified, the value specifies the number of destinations that must succeed, unless more destinations are specified as MANDATORY, in which case all MANDATORY destinations must succeed. If LOG_ARCHIVE_DEST is specified, the allowable values are 1 and 2. If this parameter is 1, LOG_ARCHIVE_DEST is a must-succeed destination, and LOG_ARCHIVE_DUPLEX_DEST is a best-effort destination. If this parameter is 2, both LOG_ARCHIVE_DEST and LOG_ARCHIVE_DUPLEX_DEST are must-succeed destinations.

If LOG_ARCHIVE_DEST or LOG_ARCHIVE_DUPLEX_DEST is specified, you cannot dynamically modify this parameter.

LOG_ARCHIVE_START

Value: TRUE | FALSE

Default: FALSE

Specifies whether archiving should be automatic or manual when the instance starts up in ARCHIVELOG mode. You can use Server Manager or the SQL*Plus commands ARCHIVE LOG START or ARCHIVE LOG STOP to override the value specified by this parameter.

To use ARCHIVELOG mode to create a database, set this parameter to TRUE. Normally, a database is created in NOARCHIVELOG mode and altered to ARCHIVELOG mode after creation.

LOG_ARCHIVE_TRACE

Value: 0 – 255

Default: 0

Dynamic: ALTER SYSTEM (changes with next archiving operation)

Specifies the level of output generated by background archiver processes into the alert file. The values for the parameter are:

0 Disables ARCHIVELOG tracing; log only errors.

1 Tracks archival of redo log file.

2 Tracks archival status of each ARCHIVELOG destination.

4 Tracks archival operational phase.

8 Tracks ARCHIVELOG destination activity.

16 Tracks detailed ARCHIVELOG destination activity.

32 Tracks ARCHIVELOG destination parameter modifications.

64 Tracks ARC*n* process state activity.

128 Tracks Fetch Archive Log (FAL) server-related activities.

These tracing levels may be combined by adding together the values corresponding to the desired levels. For example, if you want to trace the archiving of the redo log file (1) and the archive status of each ARCHIVELOG destination (2), you would specify a value of 3. New with Oracle9*i*.

LOG_BLOCK_CHECKSUM

Value: TRUE | FALSE

Default: FALSE

Specifies whether redo log blocks will include a checksum. Obsolete with Oracle9*i*.

LOG_BUFFER

Value: 2048 – 512K

Default: Operating system dependent

Specifies the amount of memory (in bytes) that is used when buffering redo entries to a redo log file. In general, larger values for LOG_BUFFER reduce redo log file I/O, particularly if transactions are long or numerous. If the system contains multiple CPUs, this value may be as high as 128K * CPU_COUNT or 512K, whichever is lower.

LOG_CHECKPOINT_INTERVAL

Value: 0 – unlimited

Default: Operating system dependent

Dynamic: ALTER SYSTEM

Specifies the frequency of checkpoints in terms of the number of redo log file operating-system blocks that are written between consecutive checkpoints. If the value exceeds the actual redo log file size, checkpoints occur only when switching logs. If the intervals are so close together that the checkpoint requests are arriving faster than the rate at which the server can satisfy them, Oracle may ignore some of these requests to avoid excessive checkpointing activity.

LOG_CHECKPOINT_TIMEOUT

Value: 0 – unlimited

Default: 0

Dynamic: ALTER SYSTEM

Specifies the maximum amount of time (in seconds) before another checkpoint occurs. The time begins at the start of the previous checkpoint.

LOG_CHECKPOINTS_TO_ALERT

Value: TRUE | FALSE

Default: FALSE

Dynamic: ALTER SYSTEM

Specifies that checkpoints be logged to the alert file. This parameter is useful in determining whether checkpoints are occurring at the desired frequency.

LOG_FILE_NAME_CONVERT

Value: List of strings (see description)

Default: None

Provides pairs of filenames that convert the filename of a new log file on the primary database to the filename of a log file on the standby database (e.g., '/disk5/prod/log1','/disk5/stby/log1'). The file must exist and be writable on the standby database or the recovery process will halt with an error.

Syntax

```
LOG_FILE_NAME_CONVERT =
   [(]'string1','string2'[,'string1','string2'...][)]
```

Keywords

string1
> Pattern found in the log file names on the primary database.

string2
> Pattern found in the log file names on the standby database.

LOGMNR_MAX_PERSISTENT_SESSIONS

Value: 1– unlimited

Default: 1

Specifies the maximum number of persistent LogMiner sessions that are concurrently active. In a clustered environment, you should set the value for the number of nodes in the cluster. New with Oracle9*i*.

MAX_COMMIT_PROPAGATION_DELAY

Value: 0 – 90000

Default: 90000

Specifies the maximum amount of time (in hundredths of seconds) allowed before the System Change Number (SCN) held in the SGA of an instance is refreshed by LGWR. It determines whether the local SCN should be refreshed from the lock value when getting the snapshot SCN for a query.

You should change this parameter only under a limited set of circumstances specific to Oracle Parallel Server. It must be identical for all nodes in the cluster.

MAX_DISPATCHERS

Value: 1 – number of dispatchers

Default: 5

Specifies the maximum number of dispatcher processes allowed to run simultaneously and applies only if dispatchers have been configured. You should set this parameter to at least the maximum number of concurrent sessions divided by the number of connections for each dispatcher. New with Oracle9i.

MAX_DUMP_FILE_SIZE

Value: 0 – unlimited

Default: Unlimited

Dynamic: ALTER SYSTEM, ALTER SESSION

Specifies the maximum size of trace files (in operating sytem blocks) to be written. You can include either a numeric value or a number followed by the suffix K or M.

MAX_ENABLED_ROLES

Value: 0 – 148

Default: 20

Specifies the maximum number of database roles that a user can enable in addition to her own role and the PUBLIC role.

MAX_ROLLBACK_SEGMENTS

Value: 2 – 65535

Default: MAX (30, TRANSACTION / TRANSACTIONS_
                PER_ROLLBACK_SEGMENT)

Specifies the maximum size of the rollback segment cache in the SGA, which also signifies the maximum number of rollback segments that can be kept online simultaneously by one instance.

MAX_SHARED_SERVERS

Value:　　　0 – 65535

Default:　　2 * SHARED_SERVERS

Specifies the maximum number of Shared Server processes that can run simultaneously.

MAX_TRANSACTION_BRANCHES

Value:　　　1 – 32

Default:　　8

Controls the number of branches in a distributed transaction, allowing up to 32 servers or server groups per instance to work on one distributed transaction.

MTS_CIRCUITS

Value:　　　Integer

Default:　　See description

Specifies the total number of virtual circuits available for network connections in a Multi-Threaded Server environment. The default is the value of SESSIONS if MTS is in use; otherwise, it is 0. New with Oracle8i. Starting with Oracle9i, use the CIRCUITS parameter instead. Obsolete with Oracle9i.

MTS_DISPATCHERS

Value:　　　String

Default:　　None

Dynamic:　　ALTER SYSTEM

Configures dispatcher processes in an MTS environment. Starting with Oracle9i, use the DISPATCHERS parameter instead. Obsolete with Oracle9i.

Syntax

```
MTS_DISPATCHERS =
'{ (PROTOCOL = protocol)
 | (ADDRESS = address)
 | (DESCRIPTION = description}
}
[({DISPATCHERS = integer
   | SESSIONS = integer
   | CONNECTIONS = integer
   | TICKS = seconds
   | POOL = {1 | ON | YES | TRUE | BOTH |({IN | OUT} = integer)|
              0 | OFF | NO | FALSE | integer}
   | MULTIPLEX = {1 | ON | YES | TRUE |
                   0 | OFF | NO | FALSE | BOTH | IN | OUT}
   | LISTENER = tnsname
   | SERVICE = service
   | INDEX = integer
})]'
```

Keywords

See the descriptions of the keywords and an example under the
DISPATCHERS parameter earlier in this section.

MTS_MAX_DISPATCHERS

Value: Greater of 5 or number of dispatchers

Default: 5

Specifies the maximum number of dispatcher processes allowed to
be running simultaneously. Starting with Oracle9*i*, use the MAX_
DISPATCHERS parameter instead. Obsolete with Oracle9*i*.

MTS_MAX_SERVERS

Value: 0 – 65535

Default: 2 * SHARED_SERVERS

Specifies the maximum number of MTS processes that can be
running simultaneously. Starting with Oracle9*i*, use the MAX_
SHARED_SERVERS parameter instead. Obsolete with Oracle9*i*.

MTS_MULTIPLE_LISTENERS

Value: TRUE | FALSE

Default: FALSE

Controls the syntax of the MTS_LISTENER_ADDRESS parameter. Obsolete with Oracle9i.

MTS_SERVERS

Value: Number of server processes

Default: 1 if using MTS, otherwise 0

Specifies the number of server processes that are to be created when an instance is started. Starting with Oracle9i, use the SHARED_SERVERS parameter instead.

MTS_SERVICE

Value: String containing service name

Default: Value of DB_NAME

Specifies the name of the service to be associated with the dispatcher. Using this name in the CONNECT string allows users to connect to an instance through a dispatcher. Make sure to specify a unique name, and do not enclose it in quotation marks. If this parameter is not specified, MTS_SERVICE defaults to the value specified by DB_NAME. If DB_NAME also is not specified, the Oracle Server returns an error at startup indicating that the value for this parameter is missing. Obsolete with Oracle9i.

NLS_CALENDAR

Value: String

Default: None

Dynamic: ALTER SESSION

Specifies the name of a calendar system to be used in this database; you can specify one of the following values:

    ARABIC HIJRAH
    ENGLISH HIJRAH
    GREGORIAN
    JAPANESE IMPERIAL

PERSIAN
ROC OFFICIAL
THAI BUDDHA

NLS_COMP

Value: BINARY | ANSI

Default: BINARY

Dynamic: ALTER SESSION

Specifies how comparisons in the WHERE clause of queries are performed. If ANSI, comparisons will use the linguistic sort specified in the NLS_SORT parameter instead of the normal binary comparison. You must have an index on the column on which you want to do a linguistic sort. New with Oracle8*i*.

NLS_CURRENCY

Value: String, up to 10 bytes

Default: Derived

Dynamic: ALTER SESSION

Specifies the string to use as the local currency symbol for the L number format element (e.g., USD). The default value is determined by NLS_TERRITORY.

NLS_DATE_FORMAT

Value: String

Default: Derived

Dynamic: ALTER SESSION

Specifies the default date format to use with the TO_CHAR and TO_DATE functions. The default value is determined by NLS_TERRITORY. The value can be any valid date format mask enclosed in double quotation marks.

NLS_DATE_LANGUAGE

Value: String

Default: Value of NLS_LANGUAGE

Dynamic: ALTER SESSION

Specifies the language to use (e.g., french) for the spelling of day and month names and date abbreviations (AD, BC, AM, PM).

NLS_DUAL_CURRENCY

Value: String

Default: Derived

Dynamic: ALTER SESSION

Specifies the dual currency symbol (e.g., EUR for the Euro) for the territory. The default value is the dual currency symbol defined in the territory of your current language environment. New with Oracle8i.

NLS_ISO_CURRENCY

Value: String

Default: Derived

Dynamic: ALTER SESSION

Specifies the name of a territory to be used to provide the international currency symbol for the C number format element (e.g., france). The default value is determined by NLS_TERRITORY.

NLS_LANGUAGE

Value: String

Default: Derived

Dynamic: ALTER SESSION

Specifies the name of the default language of the database. Used for messages; the day and month names; the symbols for AD, BC, AM, and PM; and the default sorting mechanism. This parameter determines the default values of the parameters NLS_DATE_ LANGUAGE and NLS_SORT. For a complete list of languages,

---

see the *Oracle9i Globalization Support Guide, Oracle Server Reference Manual*, and appropriate server release notes.

NLS_LENGTH_SEMANTICS

Value: BYTE | CHAR

Default: BYTE

Dynamic: ALTER SYSTEM, ALTER SESSION

Specifies whether CHAR and VARCHAR2 columns are created with byte or character-length semantics. Tables created by SYS and SYSTEM always use byte semantics. NCHAR, NVARCHAR, CLOB, and NCLOB columns are always character-based. New with Oracle9i.

NLS_NUMERIC_CHARACTERS

Value: See description

Default: Derived

Dynamic: ALTER SESSION

Specifies the characters to use as the group separator and decimal. This parameter setting overrides those defined implicitly by NLS_TERRITORY.

The two characters specified must be single-byte, and the characters must be different from each other. The characters cannot be any numeric character or any of the following characters: +, -, <, or >. The characters are specified in the following format:

```
NLS_NUMERIC_CHARACTERS=
    "<decimal_character><group_separator>"
```

NLS_SORT

Value: BINARY or string

Default: Derived

Dynamic: ALTER SESSION

Specifies the collating sequence for ORDER BY queries. If the value is BINARY, the collating sequence for ORDER BY queries is based on the numeric value of characters (a binary sort that requires less system overhead than a language sort).

If the value is a named language, sorting is based on the order of the defined linguistic sort. The default value of this parameter depends on the value of the NLS_LANGUAGE parameter. The NLS_SORT operator must be used with comparison operations if the linguistic sort behavior is desired.

Setting NLS_SORT to anything other than BINARY causes a sort to use a full table scan, regardless of the path chosen by the optimizer.

NLS_TERRITORY

Value: String

Default: Operating system dependent

Dynamic: ALTER SESSION

Specifies the name of a territory (e.g., france) whose conventions will be followed for day and week numbering, default date format, default decimal character and group separator, and default ISO and local currency symbols. For a list of territories, see the *Oracle9i Globalization Support Guide* or *Oracle Server Reference Manual*.

NLS_TIMESTAMP_FORMAT

Value: String

Default: Derived

Dynamic: ALTER SESSION

Specifies the default timestamp format (e.g., 'YYYY-MM-DD HH24: MI') to use with the TO_CHAR and TO_TIMESTAMP_TZ functions. You must enclose this value in single quotes. The default value is determined by NLS_TERRITORY. New with Oracle9i.

NLS_TIMESTAMP_TZ_FORMAT

Value: String

Default: Derived

Dynamic: ALTER SESSION

Specifies the default timestamp with time zone format (e.g., 'YYYY-MM-DD HH:MI:SS.FF TZH:TZM') to use with the TO_CHAR and TO_TIMESTAMP functions. You must enclose this value in single quotes. The default value is determined by NLS_TERRITORY. New with Oracle9i.

07_DICTIONARY_ACCESSIBILITY

Value: TRUE | FALSE

Default: FALSE

Controls restrictions on SYSTEM privileges. If the value is TRUE, access to objects in the SYS schema is allowed (Oracle7 behavior). If the value is FALSE, SYSTEM privileges that allow access to objects in other schemas do not allow access to objects in the dictionary schema. Prior to Oracle9*i*, the default for this parameter was TRUE.

OBJECT_CACHE_MAX_SIZE_PERCENT

Value: 0 – operating system dependent

Default: 10

Dynamic: ALTER SYSTEM DEFERRED, ALTER SESSION

Specifies the percentage of the optimal cache size that the session object cache can grow past the optimal size. The maximum size is equal to the optimal size plus the product of this percentage and the optimal size. When the cache size exceeds this maximum size, the system will attempt to shrink the cache to it.

OBJECT_CACHE_OPTIMAL_SIZE

Value: 102400 – operating system dependent

Default: 102400

Dynamic: ALTER SYSTEM, ALTER SESSION

Specifies the size to which the session object cache is reduced when the size of the cache exceeds the maximum size.

OPEN_CURSORS

Value: 1 – 4294967297

Default: 50

Specifies the maximum number of open cursors a session can have at once, preventing a session from opening an excessive number of cursors. No additional overhead is incurred by setting this value too high. This parameter also constrains the size of the PL/SQL cursor cache used to avoid having to reparse statements.

OPEN_LINKS

Value: 0 – 255

Default: 4

Specifies the maximum number of concurrent open connections to remote databases in one session. The value should equal or exceed the number of databases referred to in a single SQL statement that references multiple databases so that all the databases can be open to execute the statement. Can also avoid the overhead of reopening database links in sequential access.

OPEN_LINKS_PER_INSTANCE

Value: 0 – 4294967297

Default: 4

Specifies the maximum number of migratable open connections. XA transactions use migratable open connections so that the connections are cached after a transaction is committed. OPEN_LINKS_PER_INSTANCE differs from the OPEN_LINKS parameter in that OPEN_LINKS indicates the number of connections from a session and is not applicable to XA applications.

OPTIMIZER_FEATURES_ENABLE

Value: 8.0.0 | 8.0.3 | 8.0.4 | 8.0.5 | 8.0.6 | 8.1.0 | 8.1.3 | 8.1.4 | 8.1.5 | 8.1.6 | 8.1.7 | 9.0.0 | 9.0.1 | 9.2.0 | 10.0.0

Default: Current release

Specifies the behavior of the Oracle optimizer based on features available in specific release numbers.

OPTIMIZER_INDEX_CACHING

Value: 0 – 100

Default: 0

Specifies an estimated percentage of index blocks that will be cached. Higher values favor the use of index-based execution plans.

OPTIMIZER_INDEX_COST_ADJ

Value: $4 - 2^{32}$

Default: 100

Dynamic: ALTER SESSION

Specifies a "discount" to the cost of index-based execution plans.

OPTIMIZER_MAX_PERMUTATIONS

Value: $4 - 2^{32}$

Default: 80000

Dynamic: ALTER SYSTEM, ALTER SESSION

Specifies the maximum number of permutations of the tables that the optimizer will consider in queries with joins. If this parameter is low, parse times for queries will be reduced at the added risk of overlooking a better execution plan. A value of 80000 means essentially no limit.

OPTIMIZER_MODE

Value: RULE | CHOOSE | FIRST_ROWS_{1 | 10 | 100 | 1000} | FIRST_ROWS | ALL_ROWS

Default: CHOOSE

Dynamic: ALTER SESSION

Specifies the behavior of the optimizer. Cost-based optimization is be used for any query that references an object with a nonzero degree of parallelism. If FIRST_ROWS_ followed by a number (1, 10, 100, 1000) is specified, the optimizer goal is to return that number of rows as quickly as possible.

OPTIMIZER_PERCENT_PARALLEL

Value: $0 - 100$

Default: 0

Dynamic: ALTER SESSION

Specifies the amount of parallelism that the optimizer uses in its cost functions. The default means that the optimizer chooses the best serial plan. A value of 100 means that the optimizer uses each object's degree of parallelism in computing the cost of a full table scan operation. Obsolete with Oracle9*i*.

OPTIMIZER_SEARCH_LIMIT

Value: 0 – 10

Default: 5

Dynamic: ALTER SESSION

Specifies the number of tables for which Cartesian products are considered during join operations. Obsolete with Oracle9*i*.

ORACLE_TRACE_COLLECTION_NAME

Value: String

Default: None

Specifies the Oracle Trace collection name (maximum of 16 characters). This parameter is also used in the output filenames of the collection definition file *.cdf* and the datafile *.dat*, along with the ORACLE_TRACE_COLLECTION_PATH parameter.

ORACLE_TRACE_COLLECTION_PATH

Value: String

Default: operating system dependent

Specifies the fully qualified directory in which Oracle Trace collection definition and datafiles are located.

ORACLE_TRACE_COLLECTION_SIZE

Value: 0 – 4294967295

Default: 5242880

Specifies the maximum size (in bytes) of the Oracle Trace collection file. Once the collection file reaches this maximum, the collection is disabled.

ORACLE_TRACE_ENABLE

Value: TRUE | FALSE

Default: FALSE

Dynamic: ALTER SYSTEM, ALTER SESSION

Specifies whether the Oracle Trace collections for the server should be enabled. If TRUE, does not start an Oracle Trace collection but allows Oracle Trace to be used for that server. Oracle Trace can then be started in one of these ways:

- Using the Oracle Trace Manager application with the Oracle Enterprise Manager Diagnostic Pack
- Using the Oracle Trace command-line interface
- Specifying a name in the ORACLE_TRACE_COLLECTION_NAME parameter

ORACLE_TRACE_FACILITY_NAME

Value: ORACLED | ORACLEE | ORACLESM | ORACLEC

Default: ORACLED

Specifies the Oracle Trace facility product definition file (*.fdf*). The file must be located in the directory pointed to by the ORACLE_TRACE_FACILITY_PATH parameter. The product definition file contains definition information for all the events and data items that can be collected for a product that uses the Oracle Trace Data Collection API. The available product definition files are:

    ORACLE
    ORACLED
    ORACLEE
    ORACLESM
    ORACLEC
    The ALL event set
    The DEFAULT event set
    The EXPERT event set
    The SUMMARY event set
    The CACHEIO event set

ORACLE_TRACE_FACILITY_PATH

Value: String

Default: Operating system dependent

Specifies the fully qualified directory in which Oracle Trace facility product definition files are located.

OS_AUTHENT_PREFIX

Value: String

Default: OPS$

Specifies the prefix that is concatenated to the beginning of every user's operating system username to allow Oracle to authenticate users with the user's operating system account name and password. The value of this prefixed username is compared with the Oracle usernames in the database when a connection request is attempted. This mechanism has no effect for Oracle accounts that are not created using the IDENTIFIED EXTERNALLY keywords.

OS_ROLES

Value: TRUE | FALSE

Default: FALSE

Specifies whether Oracle allows the operating system to identify a user's roles. If the value is TRUE, when a user attempts to create a session, the user's security domain is initialized using the roles identified by the operating system. In addition, if TRUE, the operating system completely manages the role grants for all database users. Any revokes by the database (via SQL) of roles granted by the operating system are ignored, and any roles previously granted by the database are ignored. If the value is FALSE, roles are identified and managed by the database.

PARALLEL_ADAPTIVE_MULTI_USER

Value: TRUE | FALSE

Default: Derived

Dynamic: ALTER SYSTEM

Specifies whether Oracle will dynamically adjust the requested degree of parallelism based on the system load at the time the query begins execution. The default is taken from the value of the PARALLEL_AUTOMATIC_TUNING parameter. The algorithm used assumes that the system is tuned for optimal performance in a single-user environment.

PARALLEL_AUTOMATIC_TUNING

Value: TRUE | FALSE

Default: FALSE

Specifies whether Oracle will choose the default values for most parallel tuning parameters.You must also specify the PARALLEL clause for the target tables in the system. New with Oracle8*i*.

PARALLEL_BROADCAST_ENABLED

Value: TRUE | FALSE

Default: FALSE

Dynamic: ALTER SESSION

Specifies whether Oracle can choose to copy all the source rows of the small result set and broadcast a copy to each cluster database that is processing rows from the larger set, when applicable.

PARALLEL_DEFAULT_MAX_INSTANCES

Value: 0 – number of instances

Default: Operating system dependent

Specifies the default number of instances to split a table across for parallel query processing. Used if INSTANCES DEFAULT is specified in the PARALLEL clause of a table's definition. New with Oracle8*i*.

PARALLEL_EXECUTION_MESSAGE_SIZE

Value: 2148 – 65535

Default: Operating system dependent

Specifies the size (in bytes) of messages for parallel execution. On most systems, the default is 2148 if PARALLEL_AUTOMATIC_TUNING is FALSE and 4096 if it is TRUE. Multiple instances must have the same value. Larger values result in better performance at the cost of higher memory use.

PARALLEL_INSTANCE_GROUP

Value: String

Default: Group of all instances currently active

Identifies the parallel instance group to be used for spawning parallel query slaves. Parallel operations will spawn parallel query slaves only on instances that specify a matching group in their INSTANCE_GROUPS parameter.

PARALLEL_MAX_SERVERS

Value: 0 – 3599

Default: Derived

Specifies the maximum number of parallel query servers or parallel recovery processes for an instance. Oracle will increase the number of query servers to this value, as demand requires, from the number created at instance startup. If the value is too low, some queries may not have a query server available during query processing. If it is too high, memory resource shortages may occur during peak periods. Multiple instances must have the same value.

PARALLEL_MIN_PERCENT

Value: 0 – 100

Default: 0

Dynamic: ALTER SESSION

Specifies the minimum percent of threads required for parallel execution. Ensures that a parallel operation will not be executed sequentially if adequate resources are not available. If too few query slaves are available, an error message is displayed and the query is not executed.

PARALLEL_MIN_SERVERS

Value: 0 – PARALLEL_MAX_SERVERS

Default: 0

Specifies the minimum number of parallel execution server processes for an instance.

PARALLEL_SERVER

Value: TRUE | FALSE

Default: FALSE

Specifies that the Oracle Parallel Server option is to be enabled for this instance. Multiple instances must have the same value. Obsolete with Oracle9i.

PARALLEL_THREADS_PER_CPU

Value: 0 – unlimited

Default: Operating system dependent (usually 2)

Dynamic: ALTER SYSTEM

Specifies the default degree of parallelism for the instance and represents the number of parallel execution processes that a CPU can handle during parallel execution or in a multiple instance environment. In general, you should reduce the value if the machine appears to be overloaded when a typical parallel operation is executed, and you should increase it if the system is I/O-bound.

PARTITION_VIEW_ENABLED

Value: TRUE | FALSE

Default: FALSE

Specifies optimizer behavior for partitioned views. If TRUE, the optimizer prunes or skips unnecessary table accesses in a partition view. It also changes the way the cost-based optimizer computes statistics on a partition view from statistics on underlying tables.

PGA_AGGREGATE_TARGET

Value: 10 MB – 4000 GB

Default: 0

Specifies the target aggregate Program Global Area (PGA) memory available to all server processes attached to the instance. This parameter must be set to enable automatic sizing of SQL working areas used by memory-intensive SQL operators. New with Oracle9*i*.

PLSQL_CODE_TYPE

Value: INTERPRETED | NATIVE

Default: INTERPRETED

Dynamic: ALTER SYSTEM, ALTER SESSION

Specifies the compilation mode for PL/SQL library units. INTER-PRETED means that PL/SQL library units are compiled to PL/SQL bytecode format. Such modules are executed by the PL/SQL interpreter engine. NATIVE means that PL/SQL library units (with the possible exception of top-level anonymous PL/SQL blocks) are compiled to native (machine) code. Such modules are executed natively without incurring any interpreter overhead.

When the value of this parameter is changed, it has no effect on PL/SQL library units that have already been compiled. The value of this parameter is stored persistently with each library unit. If a PL/SQL library unit is compiled native, all subsequent automatic recompilations of that library unit will use native compilation. New with Oracle Database 10*g*.

PLSQL_COMPILER_FLAGS

Value: DEBUG | NON_DEBUG
                [INTERPRETED | NATIVE]

Default: NON_DEBUG INTERPRETED

Dynamic: ALTER SYSTEM, ALTER SESSION

Specifies compiler flags associated with PL/SQL modules. This parameter has no effect on compiled PL/SQL modules. New with Oracle9*i*.

Keywords

DEBUG
> PL/SQL modules are compiled with PROBE debug symbols.

NON_DEBUG
> PL/SQL modules are compiled without PROBE debug symbols.

INTERPRETED
> PL/SQL modules are compiled to PL/SQL bytecode format. Such modules are executed by the PL/SQL interpreter engine.

NATIVE
> PL/SQL modules (with the possible exception of top-level anonymous PL/SQL blocks) are compiled to native (machine) code. Such modules are executed natively without incurring any interpreter overhead.

PLSQL_DEBUG

Value: TRUE | FALSE

Default: FALSE

Dynamic: ALTER SYSTEM, ALTER SESSION

Specifies whether or not PL/SQL library units will be compiled for debugging. TRUE means that PL/SQL library units will be compiled for debugging, and FALSE means that PL/SQL library units will be compiled for normal execution. When this parameter is set to TRUE, PL/SQL library units are always compiled INTERPRETED in order to be debuggable. Note that when the value of this parameter is changed, it has no effect on PL/SQL library units that have already been compiled. The value of this parameter is stored persistently with each library unit. New with Oracle Database 10*g*.

PLSQL_LOAD_WITHOUT_COMPILE

Value: TRUE | FALSE

Default: FALSE

Dynamic: ALTER SESSION

Specifies whether PL/SQL can be loaded without being compiled. Obsolete with Oracle9i.

PLSQL_NATIVE_C_COMPILER

Value: String

Default: In shipped make file

Dynamic: ALTER SYSTEM

Specifies the fully qualified directory name for the C compiler that compiles generated C code into an object file. New with Oracle9*i*.

PLSQL_NATIVE_LIBRARY_DIR

Value: String

Default: None

Dynamic: ALTER SYSTEM

Specifies the fully qualified directory that stores the shared objects produced by the native compiler. New with Oracle9*i*.

PLSQL_NATIVE_LIBRARY_SUBDIR_COUNT

Value: $0 - 2^{32} - 1$

Default: 0

Dynamic: ALTER SYSTEM

Specifies the number of subdirectories created by the DBA in the directory specified by PLSQL_NATIVE_LIBRARY_DIR. Allows multiple subdirectories to be created to avoid creating a large number of files in a single directory, which can adversely affect performance. New with Oracle9*i*.

PLSQL_NATIVE_LINKER

Value: String

Default: In shipped make file

Dynamic: ALTER SYSTEM

Specifies the fully qualified directory name for the linker used to link an object file into a shared object file or DLL. New with Oracle9*i*.

PLSQL_NATIVE_MAKE_UTILITY

Value: String

Default: None

Dynamic: ALTER SYSTEM

Specifies the fully qualified directory name for the make utility used to generate a shared object file or DLL from generated C code. New with Oracle9*i*.

PLSQL_OPTIMIZE_LEVEL

Value: 0 – 2

Default: 0

Dynamic: ALTER SYSTEM, ALTER SESSION

Specifies the optimization level that will be used to compile PL/SQL library units. The higher the setting, the more effort the compiler makes to optimize PL/SQL library units. The value of this parameter is stores persistently with the library unit. New with Oracle Database 10g. The values for the parameter are:

0   Maintains the evaluation order and hence the pattern of side effects, exceptions, and package initializations of Oracle9*i* and earlier releases. Also removes the new semantic identity of BINARY_INTEGER and PLS_INTEGER and restores the earlier rules for the evaluation of integer expressions. Although code runs somewhat faster than it did in Oracle9*i*, use of level 0 forfeits most of the performance gains of PL/SQL in Oracle Database 10g.

1   Applies a wide range of optimizations to PL/SQL programs, including the elimination of unnecessary computations and exceptions, but generally does not move source code out of its original source order.

2   Applies a wide range of modern optimization techniques beyond those of level 1, including changes which may move source code relatively far from its original location.

PLSQL_V2_COMPATIBILITY

Value:	TRUE | FALSE
Default:	FALSE
Dynamic:	ALTER SYSTEM, ALTER SESSION

Sets the compatibility level for PL/SQL. If FALSE, PL/SQL Version 8 behavior is enforced, and Version 2 behavior is not allowed. If TRUE, the following PL/SQL Version 2 behaviors are accepted when running PL/SQL Version 8:

- Allows elements of an index table passed in as an IN parameter to be modified or deleted.
- Allows OUT parameters to be used in expression contexts. This behavior is restricted to a few cases: fields of OUT parameters that are records and OUT parameters referenced in the FROM list of a SELECT statement.
- Allows OUT parameters in the FROM clause of a select list, where their values are read.
- Allows the passing of an IN parameter into another procedure as an OUT parameter restricted to fields of IN parameters that are records.
- Allows a type to be referenced earlier than its definition in the source.

PLSQL_WARNINGS

Value:	See description
Default:	DISABLE:ALL
Dynamic:	ALTER SYSTEM, ALTER SESSION

Enables or disables the reporting of warning messages by the PL/SQL compiler and specifies which warning messages to show as errors. Multiple value clauses may be specified, enclosed in quotes and separated by commas. New with Oracle Database 10g.

Syntax

```
PLSQL_WARNINGS = { ENABLE | DISABLE | ERROR }:
    { ALL | SEVERE | INFORMATIONAL | PERFORMANCE |
```

```
    { integer | (integer [, integer …])}
[; PLSQL_WARNINGS = …]
```

Keywords

ENABLE

Enables a specific warning or a set of warnings.

DISABLE

Disables a specific warning or a set of warnings.

ERROR

Treats a specific warning or a set of warnings as errors.

ALL

Applies the qualifier to all warning messages.

SEVERE

Applies the qualifier to only those warning messages in the SEVERE category.

INFORMATIONAL

Applies the qualifier to only those warning messages in the INFORMATIONAL category.

PERFORMANCE

Applies the qualifier to only those warning messages in the PERFORMANCE category.

PRE_PAGE_SGA

Value: TRUE | FALSE

Default: FALSE

Specifies whether Oracle touches all of the SGA pages during instance startup, causing them to be brought into memory. Setting this parameter to TRUE increases instance startup time and user login time, but it can reduce the number of page faults that occur subsequently, which allows the instance to reach its maximum performance capability more quickly. This parameter is most useful on systems that have sufficient memory to hold all the SGA pages without degrading performance in other areas. You should ensure that the SGA is sized properly in relation to existing physical memory to avoid swapping.

PROCESSES

Value: 6 – operating system dependent

Default: Derived

Specifies the maximum number of operating-system user processes that can simultaneously connect to an Oracle server. In calculating this number, make sure to allow for all background processes, including LCK, job queue, and parallel query processes. The default value is derived from the PARALLEL_MAX_SERVERS parameter. The default value of SESSIONS is derived from the PROCESSES parameter, so if you alter it, you may also need to adjust the value of SESSIONS.

QUERY_REWRITE_ENABLED

Value: TRUE | FALSE

Default: FALSE

Dynamic: ALTER SYSTEM, ALTER SESSION

Specifies whether query rewrites of materialized views are enabled globally for the database. To take advantage of query rewrites, you must enable this option for each materialized view, and you must enable cost-based optimization. New with Oracle9*i*.

QUERY_REWRITE_INTEGRITY

Value: STALE_TOLERATED | TRUSTED | ENFORCED

Default: ENFORCED

Dynamic: ALTER SYSTEM, ALTER SESSION

Specifies the degree to which Oracle enforces query rewriting.

Keywords

STALE_TOLERATED

Allows rewrites using unenforced relationships. Materialized views may be rewritten even if they are known to be inconsistent with underlying detail data.

TRUSTED

Allows rewrites using relationships that have been declared but not enforced by Oracle.

ENFORCED
> Allows rewrites using only relationships for which Oracle enforces and guarantees consistency and integrity.

RDBMS_SERVER_DN

Value: Any X500 distinguished name

Default: None

Specifies the distinguished name (DN) of the server in order to retrieve roles for an enterprise directory service. Do not set this parameter if you want SSL authentication alone. New with Oracle9*i*.

READ_ONLY_OPEN_DELAYED

Value: TRUE | FALSE

Default: FALSE

Specifies when tables in read-only tablespaces are accessed. If TRUE, datafiles are opened only when an attempt is made to read from them. If FALSE, files are opened at database open time.

RECOVERY_PARALLELISM

Value: 0 – PARALLEL_MAX_SERVERS

Default: operating system dependent

Specifies the number of processes that participate in instance or media recovery. New with Oracle9*i*.

REMOTE_ARCHIVE_ENABLE

Value: TRUE | FALSE

Default: TRUE

Specifies whether to allow the archiving of redo logs to remote destinations. New with Oracle9*i*.

REMOTE_DEPENDENCIES_MODE

Value: TIMESTAMP | SIGNATURE

Default: TIMESTAMP

Specifies how dependencies on remote stored procedures are handled by the database. If set to TIMESTAMP, the client running the procedure compares the timestamp recorded on the server-side procedure with the current timestamp of the local procedure and executes the procedure only if the timestamps match. If set to SIGNATURE, the procedure can execute as long as the signatures are considered safe, which allows client PL/SQL applications to be run without recompilation.

REMOTE_LISTENER

Value: String

Default: None

Specifies a network name that resolves to an address or address list of Oracle network remote listeners, as specified in the *tnsnames.ora* file (e.g., test.world). New with Oracle9i.

REMOTE_LOGIN_PASSWORDFILE

Value: NONE | EXCLUSIVE | SHARED

Default: NONE

Specifies whether Oracle checks for a password file and how many databases can use the password file. Multiple instances must have the same value.

Keywords

NONE
  Indicates that Oracle should ignore any password file, which means that privileged users must be authenticated by the operating system.

EXCLUSIVE
  Indicates that the password file can be used by only one database and that the password file can contain names other than SYS and INTERNAL.

SHARED
  Allows more than one database to use a password file, but the only users recognized are SYS and INTERNAL.

REMOTE_OS_AUTHENT

Value: TRUE | FALSE

Default: FALSE

Allows authentication of remote clients using the value specified for the OS_AUTHENT_PREFIX parameter when TRUE.

REMOTE_OS_ROLES

Value: TRUE | FALSE

Default: FALSE

Allows operating-system roles for remote clients when set to TRUE.

REPLICATION_DEPENDENCY_TRACKING

Value: TRUE | FALSE

Default: TRUE

Specifies dependency tracking for read/write operations to the database. Dependency tracking is essential for the Replication Server to propagate changes in parallel. TRUE enables dependency tracking. FALSE allows read/write operations to the database to run faster but does not produce dependency information that allows the Replication Server to perform parallel propagations. Do not specify this parameter unless applications will perform absolutely no read/write operations to replicated tables.

RESOURCE_LIMIT

Value: TRUE | FALSE

Default: FALSE

Dynamic: ALTER SYSTEM

Specifies the enforcement status of resource limits set in database profiles.

RESOURCE_MANAGER_PLAN

Value: String

Default: None

Dynamic: ALTER SYSTEM

Specifies the name of the top-level resource plan for use with the instance. If this parameter is not specified, the Resource Manager is off by default.

RESUMABLE_TIMEOUT

Value: $0 - 2^{31} - 1$

Default: 0

Dynamic: ALTER SYSTEM, ALTER SESSION

Enables or disables resumable statements and specifies resumable timeout (in seconds) at the system level. New with Oracle Database 10*g*.

ROLLBACK_SEGMENTS

Value: Comma-separated list of rollback segment names (except SYSTEM)

Default: NULL

Specifies one or more rollback segments to allocate by name to this instance. If this parameter is set, an instance acquires all the rollback segments named in this parameter, even if the number of rollback segments exceeds the minimum number required by the instance (calculated from the ratio TRANSACTIONS / TRANSACTIONS_PER_ROLLBACK_SEGMENT). You can specify public rollback segments if they are not already in use. If this parameter is not set, the instance uses all public rollback segments by default. Multiple instances must have their own rollback segments.

ROW_LOCKING

Value: ALWAYS | DEFAULT | INTENT

Default: ALWAYS

Specifies whether row locks are acquired when a table is updated. ALWAYS or DEFAULT means that only row locks are acquired when a table is updated. INTENT means that only row locks are used for the SELECT portion of SELECT FOR UPDATE, but at update time, table locks are acquired.

SERIAL_REUSE

Value: DISABLE | SELECT | DML | PLSQL | ALL | NULL

Default: DISABLE

Specifies which types of SQL cursors should use the serially reusable memory features. Setting this parameter moves well-structured private cursor memory into the SGA shared pool so that it can be reused by sessions executing the same cursor.

Keywords

DISABLE

Disables the option for all SQL statement types. This value overrides any other values included in the list.

SELECT

Enables the option for SELECT statements.

DML

Enables the option for DML statements.

PLSQL

Currently has no effect.

ALL

Enables the option for both DML and SELECT statements.

NULL

Equivalent to DISABLE.

SERVICE_NAMES

Value: List of strings

Default: Value of DB_NAME.DB_DOMAIN

Dynamic: ALTER SYSTEM

Specifies one or more names (separated by commas) for the database service to which this instance connects. If the service name is not qualified with a domain, the value of the DB_DOMAIN parameter, if set, is used; otherwise, the domain of the local database as defined in the data dictionary is used. This parameter must be set for every multiple instance. New with Oracle8*i*.

SESSION_CACHED_CURSORS

Value: 0 – operating system dependent

Default: 0

Dynamic: ALTER SYSTEM

Specifies the maximum number of session cursors to keep in the session cursor cache. Repeated parse calls of the same SQL statement cause the session cursor for that statement to be moved into the session cursor cache. Subsequent parse calls need not reopen the cursor.

SESSION_MAX_OPEN_FILES

Value: 1 – the smaller of 50 or MAX_OPEN_FILES

Default: 10

Specifies the maximum number of BFILEs that can be opened in any given session. Once this number is reached, subsequent attempts to open more files in the session will fail. This parameter is also dependent on the equivalent parameter defined for the underlying operating system.

SESSIONS

Value: 1 - 2^{31}

Default: 11 * PROCESSES + 5

Specifies the total number of user and system sessions to allow. The default values of the ENQUEUE_RESOURCES and TRANSACTIONS parameters are derived from SESSIONS. If you alter the value of SESSIONS, you may also need to adjust the values for those other parameters. With the Shared Server or Multi-Threaded Server, you should set the value of SESSIONS to approximately 1.1 * (*total number of connections*).

SGA_MAX_SIZE

Value: 1 – operating system dependent

Default: Initial size of SGA at startup

Specifies the maximum size (in bytes) for the SGA during the life of the instance. New with Oracle9i.

SGA_TARGET

Value: Integer [K | M | G]

Default: 0

Dynamic: ALTER SYSTEM, ALTER SESSION

Specifies the total size of all SGA components and controls whether automatic SGA tuning is performed. If SGA_TARGET is specified, the following memory pools are automatically sized by Automatic Shared Memory Management (ASMM):

    Buffer cache (DB_CACHE_SIZE)
    Shared pool (SHARED_POOL_SIZE)
    Large pool (LARGE_POOL_SIZE)
    Java pool (JAVA_POOL_SIZE)

If the parameters corresponding to these automatically tuned memory pools are set to nonzero values, those values are used as minimum levels by ASMM. The following pools are always manually sized components and are not affected by ASMM:

    Log buffer
    Other buffer caches, such as KEEP, RECYCLE, and other
        block sizes
    Streams pool
    Fixed SGA and other internal allocations

The memory allocated to these pools is deducted from the total available for SGA_TARGET when ASMM computes the values of the automatically tuned memory pools. New with Oracle Database 10g.

SHADOW_CORE_DUMP

Value: FULL | PARTIAL

Default: PARTIAL

Determines whether the SGA will be included in core dumps. If FULL, the SGA is included in the core dump. If PARTIAL, the SGA is not dumped.

SHARED_MEMORY_ADDRESS

Value: Integer address

Default: 0

Specifies the starting address of the SGA. 0 causes the SGA address to default to a system-specific address. On 32-bit systems, this parameter is used to provide the entire address. On 64-bit platforms, this parameter is used to specify the low-order 32 bits of the address, and HI_SHARED_MEMORY_ADDRESS is used to specify the high-order 32 bits.

SHARED_POOL_RESERVED_SIZE

Value: 5000 - SHARED_POOL_SIZE / 2

Default: SHARED_POOL_SIZE * 05

Specifies the shared pool space that is reserved for large contiguous requests for shared pool memory. This parameter helps avoid performance degradation in the shared pool from situations in which pool fragmentation forces Oracle to search for and free chunks of unused pool to satisfy the current request. If SHARED_POOL_RESERVED_SIZE exceeds half the SHARED_POOL_SIZE, Oracle signals an error. In general, you should set SHARED_POOL_RESERVED_SIZE to 10% of SHARED_POOL_SIZE. This parameter can be specified as a numeric value or a number followed by K or M.

SHARED_POOL_SIZE

Value: 300K – operating system dependent

Default: 64M for 64-bit systems, otherwise 16M

Dynamic: ALTER SYSTEM

Specifies the size of the shared pool (in bytes). This parameter can be specified as a numeric value or a number followed by K (kilobytes) or M (megabytes).

SHARED_SERVER_SESSIONS

Value: 0 – SESSIONS - 5

Default: lesser of CIRCUITS or SESSIONS - 5

Specifies the total number of Shared Server user sessions. New with Oracle9*i*.

SKIP_UNUSABLE_INDEXES

Value: TRUE | FALSE

Default: TRUE

Dynamic: ALTER SYSTEM, ALTER SESSION

Specifies whether tables with unusable indexes or index partitions are used. If TRUE, error reporting of indexes and index partitions marked UNUSABLE is disabled, and all operations (inserts, deletes, updates, and selects) on tables with unusable indexes or index partitions continues. If an index is used to enforce a constraint on a table, allowing insert and update operations on the table might violate the constraint. Therefore, this setting does not disable error reporting for unusable indexes that are unique. If FALSE, error reporting of indexes marked UNUSABLE is enabled, and inserts, deletes, and updates on tables with unusable indexes or index partitions are not allowed.

SMTP_OUT_SERVER

Value: host name[:port]

Default: See description

Specifies the SMTP host and port to which the UTL_MAIL package delivers outbound email. You can specify multiple server names (separated by commas); if the first server in the list is unavailable, UTL_MAIL tries the second server, and so on (e.g., mail.acme.com:25,smtp.acme.com:35). If SMTP_OUT_SERVER is not specified, then the SMTP server name defaults to the value of the DB_DOMAIN parameter, the port number defaults to 25, and the SMTP domain defaults to the suffix of DB_DOMAIN.

SORT_AREA_RETAINED_SIZE

Value: 2 * DB_BLOCK_SIZE - SORT_AREA_SIZE

Default: SORT_AREA_SIZE

Dynamic: ALTER SYSTEM DEFERRED, ALTER SESSION

Specifies the maximum amount (in bytes) of user memory retained after a sort run completes. The retained size controls the size of the read buffer used to maintain a portion of the sort in memory. You may allocate multiple sort spaces of this size.

SORT_AREA_SIZE

Value: 6 * DB_BLOCK_SIZE – operating system dependent

Default: Operating system dependent

Dynamic: ALTER SYSTEM DEFERRED, ALTER SESSION

Specifies the maximum amount (in bytes) of PGA memory to use for a sort. If Shared Server/MTS is enabled, the sort area is allocated from the SGA. After the sort is complete, and only row-retrieval remains, memory is released to the size specified by SORT_AREA_RETAINED_SIZE. After the last row is retrieved, all memory is freed. The memory is released back to the PGA, not to the operating system.

With Oracle9*i*, Oracle recommends that you use this parameter only for an instance configured with the Shared Server option. Otherwise, Oracle recommends that you use the PGA_ AGGREGATE_TARGET parameter instead.

SPFILE

Value: String

Default: $ORACLE_HOME/dbs/spfile*sid*.ora

Specifies the name of the server parameter file (*SPFILE*) currently in use. If you have multiple instances, they should all have the same value.

SQL92_SECURITY

Value: TRUE | FALSE

Default: FALSE

Specifies whether table-level SELECT privileges are required to execute an update or delete that references table column values.

SQL_TRACE

Value: TRUE | FALSE

Default: FALSE

Disables or enables the SQL Trace facility. While not dynamically changeable using the ALTER SYSTEM or ALTER SESSION statements, SQL_TRACE can be changed using the DBMS_SYSTEM package.

SQLTUNE_CATEGORY

Value: String

Default: DEFAULT

Dynamic: ALTER SYSTEM, ALTER SESSION

Specifies the category name for use by sessions to qualify the lookup of SQL profiles during SQL compilation. New with Oracle Database 10g.

STANDBY_ARCHIVE_DEST

Value: String

Default: Operating system dependent

Dynamic: ALTER SYSTEM

Specifies the fully qualified directory or device name to be used as a destination for archived log files arriving for a standby database in managed recovery mode. New with Oracle9i.

STANDBY_FILE_MANAGEMENT

Value: MANUAL | AUTO

Default: MANUAL

Dynamic: ALTER SYSTEM

Specifies whether automatic standby file management is enabled. If AUTO, file-management operations such as adding and deleting files are performed automatically on the standby database. New with Oracle9i.

STANDBY_PRESERVES_NAMES

Value: TRUE | FALSE

Default: FALSE

Dynamic: ALTER SYSTEM

Specifies whether filenames on the standby database are the same (preserved) as those on the primary database. New with Oracle9*i*.

STAR_TRANSFORMATION_ENABLED

Value: TRUE | FALSE

Default: FALSE

Dynamic: ALTER SESSION

Determines whether a cost-based query transformation will be applied to star queries.

STREAMS_POOL_SIZE

Value: Integer [K | M | G] – operating system dependent

Default: 0

Dynamic: ALTER SYSTEM

Specifies the size of the Streams pool (in bytes). If this parameter is not specified or is set to 0, up to 10% of the shared pool is allocated for Streams. New in Oracle Database 10*g*.

THREAD

Value: 0 – maximum number of enabled threads

Default: 0

Specifies the number of the redo thread that is to be used by the instance. THREAD is applicable only to instances that intend to run with Real Application Clusters or Oracle Parallel Server. Any available redo thread number can be used, but an instance cannot use the same thread number as another instance and cannot start when its redo thread is disabled.

A value of 0 causes an available, enabled public thread to be chosen. Redo threads are specified with the THREAD option of the ALTER DATABASE ADD LOGFILE statement and enabled with the ALTER DATABASE ENABLE [PUBLIC] THREAD statement. The PUBLIC keyword signifies that the redo thread may be used by any instance. Thread 1 is the default thread in exclusive mode, but an instance running in exclusive mode can specify the THREAD keyword to use the redo log files in a thread other than thread 1.

TIMED_STATISTICS

Value: TRUE | FALSE

Default: FALSE

Dynamic: ALTER SYSTEM, ALTER SESSION

Specifies whether statistics related to time are collected. If FALSE, the statistics are always zero, and the server can avoid the overhead of requesting the time from the operating system.

TRACE_ENABLED

Value: TRUE | FALSE

Default: TRUE

Dynamic: ALTER SYSTEM, ALTER SESSION

Specifies whether tracing of the execution history or code path is performed. Multiple instances must have the same value. New with Oracle9*i*.

TRACEFILE_IDENTIFIER

Value: String

Default: None

Dynamic: ALTER SESSION

Specifies a custom identifier that becomes a part of the Oracle Trace filename for foreground processes. When used, the value provided is made a part of the trace filename using the format *sid*_ora_*pid*_*traceid*.trc, where *sid* is the Oracle instance ID, *pid* is the process ID, and *traceid* is the value provided for this parameter. New with Oracle9*i*.

TRANSACTION_AUDITING

Value: TRUE | FALSE

Default: TRUE

Dynamic: ALTER SYSTEM DEFERRED

Specifies whether the transaction layer generates a special redo record that contains session and user information.

TRANSACTIONS

Value: $4 - 2^{32}$

Default: 11 * SESSIONS

Specifies the maximum number of concurrent transactions.

TRANSACTIONS_PER_ROLLBACK_SEGMENT

Value: 1 – operating system dependent

Default: 21

Specifies the number of concurrent transactions allowed per rollback segment. The minimum number of rollback segments acquired at startup is TRANSACTIONS divided by the value for this parameter.

UNDO_MANAGEMENT

Value: MANUAL | AUTO

Default: MANUAL

Specifies which undo space management mode is used. If MANUAL, undo space is allocated as rollback segments. If AUTO, automatic undo management is used. New with Oracle9i.

UNDO_RETENTION

Value: $0 - 2^{32} - 1$

Default: 900

Dynamic: ALTER SYSTEM

Specifies (in seconds) how long committed undo information is to be retained in the database. Multiple instances must have the same value. New with Oracle9i.

UNDO_SUPPRESS_ERRORS

Value: TRUE | FALSE

Default: FALSE

Dynamic: ALTER SYSTEM, ALTER SESSION

Specifies whether errors are suppressed while executing manual undo management operations in automatic undo management mode. Used with pre-Oracle9i scripts with undo management commands used with Oracle9i.

UNDO_TABLESPACE

Value: Name of an existing undo tablespace

Default: First available undo tablespace

Dynamic: ALTER SYSTEM

Specifies the undo tablespace to be used when the instance starts. If no undo tablespace is specified or available, Oracle uses the SYSTEM rollback segment, which is not recommended. The instance will not start if a value is provided for this parameter, and the database is in manual undo management mode. New with Oracle9i.

USE_INDIRECT_DATA_BUFFERS

Value: TRUE | FALSE

Default: FALSE

Specifies how the SGA uses memory. If TRUE, enables the use of the extended buffer cache mechanism for 32-bit platforms that can support more than 4 GB of physical memory. If FALSE, this capability is disabled. New with Oracle8i.

USER_DUMP_DEST

Value: String

Default: Operating system dependent

Dynamic: ALTER SYSTEM.

Specifies the fully qualified directory name in which the server will write debugging trace files on behalf of a user process.

UTL_FILE_DIR

Value: String

Default: NULL

Specifies the fully qualified name of a directory that is permitted for PL/SQL file I/O. You can specify multiple directories, but each directory must be specified with a separate UTL_FILE_DIR parameter.

WORKAREA_SIZE_POLICY

Value: AUTO | MANUAL

Default: Derived

Dynamic: ALTER SYSTEM, ALTER SESSION

Specifies the policy for sizing work areas. If AUTO, work areas used by memory-intensive operations are sized automatically, based on the PGA memory used by the system. This value can be specified only if the PGA_AGGREGATE_TARGET parameter is defined and is the default if PGA_AGGREGATE_TARGET is defined. If MANUAL, the sizing of work areas is manual and is based on the value of the corresponding *_AREA_SIZE parameter that applies (e.g., a sort uses SORT_AREA_SIZE) to the operation being performed. MANUAL is the default if PGA_ AGGREGATE_TARGET is not defined. Obsolete with Oracle9i.

Index

We'd like to hear your suggestions for improving our indexes. Send email to
index@oreilly.com.